Scholars Prai
God's Song

Jean Griesser has made another unique contribution to our study of the spiritual traditions of South Asia. Her illustrated summary of the *Bhagavad-gita*, the single most influential text of Indian wisdom, comprehends and effectively communicates the timeless relevance of the *Gita* within a contemporary context. Her mature ability to blend her award-winning skills as a photographer with an appealing and convincing text are clearly in evidence here.

In this publication, we have an extraordinary opportunity to comprehend the *Gita* as it has been historically understood within its own sacred tradition, and yet at the same time grasp its message within a cutting-edge visual and literary picture of life as we live it today.

Howard J. Resnick, Ph.D. in Sanskrit and Indian Studies
*   from Harvard University*
Visiting Scholar in Indo-European Studies, UCLA
Adjunct Professor of Sanskrit and Indian Studies,
Graduate Theological Union, Berkeley, California

Bhagavad-gita, India's most popular and widely read religious scripture, is available in nearly two thousand different versions in almost one hundred different languages. Jean Griesser has added a further unique contribution to this illustrious ongoing commentarial heritage by blending an easy-to-read and highly accessible synopsis of the text with relevant and usefully placed photographs that highlight the essential philosophical points and make them relevant to the modern context. This version will be particularly appreciated by the non-specialized public interested in Indian spirituality.

Edwin Bryant, Ph.D.
Lecturer of Indian Studies
Harvard University

Bhagavad-gita
~India's Ancient Book of Wisdom~

FULLY ILLUSTRATED

God's Song

A Summary Study of His Divine Grace
A. C. Bhaktivedanta Swami Prabhupada's

Bhagavad-gita As It Is

BY JEAN GRIESSER

WITH ILLUSTRATIONS BY JEAN AND JOHN GRIESSER

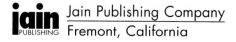 Jain Publishing Company
Fremont, California

Those who want further information on the subject matter of this book are
invited to read the *Bhagavad-gita As It Is* by His Divine Grace A. C.
Bhaktivedanta Swami Prabhupada, Founder-Acarya of the International
Society for Krishna Consciousness. This book is available from the
Bhaktivedanta Book Trust at 800-927-4152.

God's Song is published by Jain Publishing, P.O. Box 3523, Fremont, CA 94539.
Web Site: www.jainpub.com   Telephone: 510-659-8272

Library of Congress Cataloging-in-Publication Data
Griesser, Jean, 1950-
    God's song : a summary study of His Divine Grace A.C. Bhaktivedanta Swami
Prabhupada's Bhagavad-gita as it is / by Jean Griesser ; with illustrations by Jean
and John Griesser.
        p.   cm.
    At head of title: Bhagavad-gita, India's ancient book of wisdom, fully illustrated.
    ISBN 0-87573-085-X (paper : alk. paper)
    1. Bhagavadgita--Criticism, interpretation, etc.   I. A.C. Bhaktivedanta Swami
Prabhupada, 1896-1977. II. Title. III. Title: Bhagavad-gita, India's ancient book of
wisdom, fully illustrated.
BL1138.66.G74 1999
294.5'924046--dc21   99-28446 CIP

On the cover: As described by Queen Kunti, the mother of Arjuna
(the heroic prince who heard *Bhagavad-gita* from Krishna), the form,
presence, qualities, and beauty of the lotus flower all evoke remembrance
of the Supreme Lord Krishna:

"My respectful obeisances unto You, O Lord, whose abdomen is
marked with a depression like a lotus flower, who are always decorated
with garlands of lotus flowers, whose glance is as cool as the lotus and
whose feet are engraved with lotuses."

Srimad Bhagavatam 1.8.22

Dedicated to His Divine Grace A. C. Bhaktivedanta Swami Prabhupada and his followers, generous souls who forever attempt to evoke the divine within us

Some sort of fault covers every endeavor, Krishna says, and this endeavor would have been covered by many more faults had it not been for the clear-headed help of Jayadvaita Swami and Krishna-kripa Dasa, as well as my friends Bimala Devi and Lelise Folse. Also, my heartfelt gratitude to my friend and husband, John, as well as to our daughters, Amrita and Hari Priya.

In darkness we may confuse a rope for a snake because we can be overcome by illusion. Similarly, in ignorance we've accepted our body and mind as our self, but this is an illusion. A bona fide scripture like the *Bhagavad-gita* can free us from such an illusion.

Contents

As the opposing armies stand poised for battle, Arjuna, the mighty warrior, sees his intimate relatives, teachers, and friends in both armies ready to fight and sacrifice their lives. Overcome by grief and pity, Arjuna fails in strength, his mind becomes bewildered, and he gives up his determination.

Arjuna submits to Lord Krishna as His disciple, and Krishna begins His teachings to Arjuna by explaining the fundamental distinction between the temporary material body and the eternal spiritual soul. The Lord explains the process of transmigration, the nature of selfless service to the Supreme, and the characteristics of a self-realized person.

Krishna explains the meaning of renunciation and the effects of the modes of nature on human consciousness and activity. He explains Brahman* realization, the glories of the *Bhagavad-gita,* and the ultimate conclusion of the *Gita:* the highest path of religion is absolute, unconditional loving service unto Lord Krishna, which frees one from all sins, brings one to complete enlightenment, and enables one to return to Krishna's eternal spiritual abode.

*The Sanskrit word "Brahman" has several meanings, namely (1) the individual soul; (2) the impersonal, all-pervasive aspect of the Supreme; (3) the Supreme Lord; and (4) the total material substance.

Foreword

THE BHAGAVAD-GITA, OR "GOD'S SONG," is a classical sacred text that comes to us from ancient India. Indeed, the *Bhagavad-gita* is a "song" (*gita*), as its text is found in flowing Sanskrit verse. Yet, the content of this poem takes the form of a conversation between the Supreme Lord Krishna (the *bhagavat*), and his dear friend Arjuna, who is confronted by universal existential questions that continue to challenge humans: What is my purpose in life? What should be the values by which I can make critical life decisions? What constitutes true happiness and fulfillment while in a world of moral conflict and degradation? What is the ultimate reality and what is my relationship to it? These are just some of the questions to which this text poses answers.

Often called the "Hindu" Bible, the *Bhagavad-gita* is the most loved and adored philosophical text arising from the ancient culture of South Asia. This text is a 700-verse section within the largest epic poem in the world, known as the *Mahabharata*, a magnificent epic poem at least seven times the length of both Homer's *Iliad* and *Odyssey* combined! One remarkable fact about the *Bhagavad-gita* is that it has captured the minds of and has fascinated non-Indian peoples, especially in the English-speaking world. There have been literally hundreds of translations of the text published in English alone, which is evidence that the voices from ancient India are still speaking to us in modern times.

The present work, however, is a unique presentation of key philosophical ideas and understandings of this great text. The author of this work has presented select topics and themes of the text and has explained them with the aid of photographic illustrations. Specifically, she draws from the translation and commentary of the *Bhagavad-gita* by A. C. Bhaktivedanta Swami Prabhupada (1896–1977), entitled, *Bhagavad-gita As It Is*. The reasons for this choice may be considered here. One, it may be that Prabhupada's translation and commentary, distributed by the International Society for Krishna Consciousness, is the single most widely known translation in English, as well as numerous other languages. It makes sense that the present work would focus on such a celebrated translation. Two, this translation is what I would term a "living translation" of the text, in that it is not merely the philological exercise of a specialist; rather, the Swami's work was translated clearly with the idea that it would be applied in the everyday lives of persons. Indeed, the Swami's mission was itself the cause of the worldwide spread of Vaishnava thought and practice in all major cultures of the world. Finally, the author herself, Jean Griesser, a direct student of Bhaktivedanta Swami since 1971, has been practicing for many years the way of life that is prescribed in the *Bhagavad-gita* and in the Swami's commentary.

We are greatly benefitted by the way Jean Griesser brings together the areas of art and religion from her own life to create the present work. The author harnesses her talents both as an accomplished writer and as a professional photographer (originally trained at the Rochester Institute of Technology). Combined with these talents are her years of dedicated practice of *bhakti-yoga*, or the practice of living a life in loving devotion to God under the guidance of this century's leading global teacher of *Bhagavad-gita*, Bhaktivedanta Swami.

The ancient, yet universally relevant message of the *Gita* is extended to us in the modern world through Griesser's clearly articulated understanding along with her powerful photographic expression of its message. I recommend this work to devotees of the religious traditions of the *Gita* and to academic students of the *Gita*, as well as to all those who desire a glimpse into the mystical vision of the *Gita*, as it is so eloquently presented herein.

Dr. Graham M. Schweig
Specialist in South Asia Religions and
the Psychology of Religion
Department of Religion
Duke University
Durham, NC

His Divine Grace A. C. Bhaktivedanta
Swami Prabhupada, author of
Bhagavad-gita As It Is, the book
from which *God's Song* is derived.

Introduction

IN JUNE OF 1970 MY HUSBAND and I began a month-long trekking adventure near Pokra in Nepal. At the snow line—around 10,000 feet at that time of year—we found a small abandoned cowshed and decided to spend a few restful days. From deep inside his backpack, John, my husband, pulled out a blue paperback book with a line drawing of a regal-looking four-armed person on the cover. During our cowshed stay, I sat for hours surrounded by towering snowy peaks in crystal-clear air, with no humans other than the two of us for miles around, trying to read this early edition of *Bhagavad-gita As It Is*. Despite the pristine environs, I understood little. But I was intrigued. The idea of tolerating dualities and remaining equipoised in their midst enticed me, as did the concept of an eternal spiritual presence within all living beings and the thought of improving my character as well as the quality of my life through knowledge.

Over the intervening years, as I continued studying *Bhagavad-gita*, my respect for its wisdom, relevance, and comprehensiveness grew. In 1996 I wrote and illustrated a *Bhagavad-gita* for children, *Our Most Dear Friend* (Torchlight), and thereafter began this current version, *God's Song*.

God's Song does not attempt to present all 700 verses of the *Bhagavad-gita*. Rather, through the text and visuals, it presents the essential and most relevant teachings of the *Gita*, teachings that have inspired and improved my life. Thus it is called a "summary study."

Throughout the text, the speakers of the *Gita's* verses are clearly indicated, followed by the translation from Sanskrit of the verses (in quotation marks) they speak, and then by a brief commentary on those verses by A. C. Bhaktivedanta Swami Prabhupada. (On rare occasions I have incorporated part of his commentary into the verses themselves.) In this way the reader can easily follow the flow of the conversation, beginning with Arjuna's dilemma and questions, through Krishna's responses, to the ultimate realizations of both Arjuna and Sanjaya, the person who relates *Bhagavad-gita* to King Dhritarastra.

Ideas for the photographs came from both the verses of the *Gita* and the commentaries. Although some of the photographs portray the various persons involved or mentioned in the *Gita*, most illustrate philosophical points, often through analogies.

Over my years of reflection on *Bhagavad-gita*, I have found that analogies often clarify otherwise obscure philosophical concepts, vividly impress other points upon the mind, and sometimes bring a rush of understanding where previously there was none. My husband and I created some of the photographs on these pages specifically for *God's Song*. Others I culled from the files we have kept on our travels as professional photojournalists.

Bhagavad-gita offers us direction that is practical, yet sublime, and it beckons us toward something mystical and delightful, to that realm which is beyond our conception. Taken from the last instructions Krishna offers to Arjuna is an example of the practical, sublime, and mystical together: "By worship of the Lord, who is the source of all beings and who is all-pervading, persons can attain perfection through performing their own work."

An Overview of the Bhagavad-gita

BHAGAVAD-GITA, A CONVERSATION between the Supreme Lord Krishna and His devotee and friend Arjuna, takes place in a dramatic setting: a battlefield on which Arjuna and his allies are poised to fight a great war. However, when Arjuna surveys the opposing army and sees his relatives prepared to conquer him or die in the attempt, he is overcome with compassion for them and unable to fight. Yet he must fight. His relatives on the opposing side have acted immorally, illegally, and dictatorially. And they've refused all offers of peaceful reconciliation.

Krishna speaks *Bhagavad-gita* to persuade Arjuna to fight, to transform his vision from the mundane to the sublime, from the material to the spiritual. And in speaking to Arjuna, He also speaks to all of us. Just as Arjuna has difficulty in fighting, so everyone has some sort of perplexity or difficulty. By His words, Krishna enables Arjuna to transcend his difficulties and reestablish his real purpose in life.

The *Bhagavad-gita* entails five basic truths: God (the Supreme Lord), the living entities, material nature, time, and the activities of the living entities (karma).

God is the supreme controller, the greatest of all. The living entities, God's parts and parcels, have His qualities in minute quantity; they are conscious and have an intimate, eternal relationship with God. Material nature, God's inferior, separated energy, is not conscious. It's constituted of three qualities: the modes of goodness, passion and ignorance. Above these modes there is time, and by a combination of these modes of nature and under the control of time the living entities act and suffer or enjoy the results (karma).

The Supreme Lord, the living entity, material nature, and time are all interrelated and eternal. However, the other item, karma (action and reaction), is not eternal. The living entities are suffering or enjoying the results of their activities from time immemorial, but they can change their karma, and this change depends upon their knowledge.

In his introduction to the *Bhagavad-gita As It Is*, His Divine Grace A. C. Bhaktivedanta Swami Prabhupada writes, ". . . *Bhagavad-gita* should be taken up in a spirit of devotion. One should not think that he is equal to Krishna, nor should he think that Krishna is an ordinary personality or even a very great personality. Lord Sri Krishna is the Supreme Personality of Godhead. So according to the statements of *Bhagavad-gita* or the statements of Arjuna, . . . we should at least theoretically accept Sri Krishna as the Supreme Personality of Godhead, and with that submissive spirit we can understand the *Bhagavad-gita*. Unless one reads the *Bhagavad-gita* in a submissive spirit, it is very difficult to understand *Bhagavad-gita*, because it is a great mystery."

The knowledge in *Bhagavad-gita* can lead one to purify one's activities through the process of *bhakti* (loving devotional service to God). Activities in *bhakti* appear ordinary, but they are not material; they liberate one from the bodily concept of life and lead to a spirit of cooperation with the Supreme Lord. As the *Gita* ends, Arjuna accepts the path of *bhakti*.

Setting the Scene

ALTHOUGH WIDELY PUBLISHED and read by itself, *Bhagavad-gita* originally appeared as an episode in the *Mahabharata,* the epic Sanskrit history of the ancient world. The *Mahabharata* describes events leading up to the present Age of Kali. It was at the beginning of this age, some fifty centuries ago, that Lord Krishna spoke *Bhagavad-gita* to His friend and devotee Arjuna.

Their discourse—one of the most beautiful and profound texts of world literature—took place just before the onset of war, a great fratricidal conflict between the sons of Dhritarastra and their cousins, the sons of Pandu.

Dhritarastra and Pandu were brothers born into the Kuru dynasty, which descended from King Bharata, a former ruler of the earth, from whom the name *Mahabharata* derives. Because Dhritarastra, the elder brother, was born blind, the throne that otherwise would have been his went to his younger brother, Pandu.

When Pandu died at an early age, his five children—Arjuna among them—came under the care of Dhritarastra, who in effect became, for the time being, the king. Thus the sons of Dhritarastra and those of Pandu grew up in the same royal household, were trained in the military arts by the same teacher, and were counseled by the same revered "grandfather" of the clan.

Yet the sons of Dhritarastra, especially the eldest, Duryodhana, hated and envied the Pandavas (the sons of Pandu). And the blind and evil-minded Dhritarastra wanted his own sons, not those of Pandu, to inherit the kingdom.

Thus Duryodhana, with Dhritarastra's consent, plotted to kill Pandu's young sons, his cousins, and only by the careful protection of Lord Krishna did the Pandavas escape the many attempts against their lives.

Now Lord Krishna was not an ordinary man, but the Supreme Lord Himself, who had descended to earth and was playing the role of prince in a contemporary dynasty. In this role, and as the eternal upholder of religion, Krishna favored the righteous sons of Pandu.

Ultimately, however, the clever Duryodhana challenged the Pandavas to a gambling match (which was rigged), cheated them out of their kingdom, insulted their wife, and forced them into thirteen years of exile.

After their exile, the Pandavas rightfully requested the return of their kingdom from Duryodhana, who bluntly refused to yield it. Duty bound as princes to serve in public administration, the five Pandavas reduced their request to a mere five villages. But Duryodhana arrogantly replied that he wouldn't spare them even enough land into which to drive a pin.

Throughout all those years, the Pandavas had been consistently tolerant and forbearing. But now war seemed inevitable.

Nonetheless, as the kings of the world divided, some siding with the sons of Dhritarastra, others with the Pandavas, Krishna Himself took the role of messenger for the sons of Pandu and went to the court of Dhritarastra to plead for peace. When His pleas were refused, war was certain.

Krishna offered to enter the war according to the desire of the antagonists. As God, He would not personally fight; but whoever so desired might have Krishna Himself as advisor and helper—and the other side, Krishna's army. The Pandavas, men of the highest moral stature, recognized Krishna as the Supreme Lord and were eager to have the Lord Himself on their side. The impious sons of Dhritarastra, however, did not recognize Krishna as the Lord and chose instead His army.

In this way, Krishna took it upon Himself to drive the chariot of the fabled bowman, Arjuna. This brings us to the point at which *Bhagavadgita* begins, the two armies arrayed against each other, ready for combat, with King Dhritarastra anxiously inquiring of his secretary, Sanjaya, "What did they do?"

~ *God's Song* ~

1

Observing the Armies on the Battlefield

Dhritarastra asks,

"O SANJAYA, AFTER MY SONS and the sons of Pandu assembled on
the battlefield of Kurukshetra, desiring to fight, what did
they do?"

The blind Dhritarastra questions his secretary, Sanjaya, who, through
his mystic power, can see the events on the battlefield.

Sanjaya replies,
"After looking over the army gathered by the sons of Pandu, Duryodhana
went to his military teacher and said: 'Behold the great army of the sons
of Pandu . . .' "

Duryodhana, the eldest of Dhritarastra's many sons, is surprised when
he sees the military strength of the Pandavas (the sons of Pandu). Yet,
thinking of the many heroes who had come from all parts of the world
to fight on his behalf, he feels confident of victory. He asks his army to
give their full support to their general, Bhisma.

Then Bhisma, the valiant general of Duryodhana's army, "blows his
conchshell very loudly, making a sound like the roar of a lion, giving
Duryodhana joy. After that, the conchshells, drums, bugles, trumpets,
and horns all suddenly sound, and the combined sound is tumultuous."

The sounds of these instruments enliven the soldiers to fight, and
the opposing side, the Pandavas, also use them.

"On the side of the Pandavas, both Lord Krishna and Arjuna,
stationed on a great chariot drawn by white horses, sound their transcendental conchshells."

Unlike the conchshells blown by Duryodhana's army, Sanjaya describes the conchshells in the hands of Krishna and Arjuna as transcendental. Krishna is transcendental; He is not of this material world. And anything directly related to Krishna is also transcendental: His activities, associates, paraphernalia, name, and so forth. The sounding of transcendental conchshells indicates that there is no hope of victory for the other side.

Krishna, the Supreme Lord and speaker of the Bhagavad-gita.

3

Following the lead of Krishna and Arjuna, the other great warriors on the Pandava side also blow their conchshells, and the sound becomes uproarious. "Vibrating both in the sky and on the earth, it shatters the hearts of the sons of Dhritarastra." The unexpected arrangement of military force by the Pandavas, who are guided directly by Lord Krishna, disheartens Duryodhana and his allies.

Sanjaya continues,
"Arjuna, the son of Pandu, takes up his bow and prepares to shoot his arrows. O Dhritarastra, after looking at your sons, drawn in military array, Arjuna says to Krishna: 'O infallible one, please draw my chariot between the two armies so that I may see those present here who desire to fight, and with whom I must contend in this great battle.' "

Lord Krishna is playing the role of Arjuna's charioteer, and because He never fails in His affection for His devotees, Arjuna addresses Him as "infallible." In all circumstances Krishna is the Supreme Lord, but in the sweetness of His transcendental relationships with His devotees, the Lord always seeks an opportunity to serve them, as they are always ready to serve Him.

"Having thus been addressed by Arjuna, Lord Krishna draws up the fine chariot in the midst of the armies of both parties and says, 'Just behold, Arjuna, all the sons of Dhritarastra and their allies assembled here.' "

On seeing his father's friends, his grandfathers, teachers, maternal uncles, cousins, the sons and grandsons of his cousins, as well as his friends and well-wishers, Arjuna is filled with compassion.

Arjuna, Krishna's devotee and friend, who hears the Bhagavad-gita.

Arjuna says,
"My dear Krishna, seeing my friends and relatives present before me in such a fighting spirit, I feel the limbs of my body quivering and my mouth drying up. My whole body trembles, my hair stands on end, my bow slips from my hand, and my skin burns."

Practically the whole community, all the blood relatives of Arjuna, had come to fight with him. This overwhelmed a kind devotee like Arjuna.

"I cannot stand here any longer. I am forgetting myself, and my mind is reeling. I see only causes of misfortune, O Krishna. I do not see how any good can come from killing my kinsmen in this battle, nor can I, my dear Krishna, desire any subsequent victory, kingdom, or happiness.

"O maintainer of all living entities, what pleasure will we derive, what should we gain, and how could we be happy by killing the sons of Dhritarastra?"

Although the sons of Dhritarastra are overtaken by greed and blind to the evil of this war, Arjuna sees the crime in destroying a family. "With the destruction of dynasty, the family tradition is vanquished, and thus the rest of the family becomes involved in irreligion.

"Alas, how strange it is that we are preparing to commit greatly sinful acts. Driven by the desire to enjoy royal happiness, we are intent on killing our own kinsmen. Better for me if the sons of Dhritarastra kill me unarmed and unresisting on the battlefield."

Arjuna is virtuous, detached, cultured, intelligent and, most importantly, devoted to God. These qualifications make him fit to receive transcendental knowledge.

Sanjaya says,
"Arjuna, having thus spoken on the battlefield, cast aside his bow and arrows and sat down on the chariot, his mind overwhelmed with grief."

One who hears the Bhagavad-gita as Arjuna did, accepting Krishna's message as it is, will be awakened from the confusion and frustration of daily life and drawn to the majesty of the divine. This message is clear in itself and does not require interpretation, just as the sun does not require our lamp to be visible.

A dream is terrifying until the dreamer wakes up and realizes there's nothing to fear. Similarly, Arjuna's situation is hellish until he awakens from thinking of himself as the temporary material body and sees himself as a soul, eternally existing and therefore unable to be harmed. Arjuna thus realizes that while fighting under Krishna's direction he has nothing to fear. This is the essence of Krishna's teachings in Chapter Two.

2

Contents of the Gita Summarized

SEEING ARJUNA FULL OF COMPASSION, his mind depressed, and his eyes full of tears, Krishna begins to enlighten Arjuna with His philosophical teachings.

The Supreme Lord
"My dear Arjuna, how have these impurities come upon you? They are not at all befitting a person who knows the value of life. They lead only to infamy. Give up such petty weakness of heart and arise, O chastiser of the enemy."

Arjuna
"How can I fight with my grandfather and teacher, who are worthy of my worship? It would be better to live by begging than to kill them. Even though they desire worldly gain, they are superiors. If they are killed, everything we enjoy will be tainted with blood."

Arjuna turns to Lord Krishna, the supreme spiritual master, for a definitive solution to his perplexity. "Now I am confused about my duty and have lost all composure because of miserly weakness. In this condition I am asking You to tell me for certain what is best for me. Now I am Your disciple, and a soul surrendered unto You. Please instruct me."

Arjuna, chastiser of enemies, then tells Krishna, "I shall not fight," and falls silent.

Lord Krishna smiles and, in the presence of both armies, replies to the grief-stricken Arjuna. God's song is not for any particular person, society,

The differences between one frame of movie film and another are so minuscule that at first glance the frames all look alike. But when the film is projected, we see the illusion of a continuous image. Similarly, though from moment to moment we transmigrate from one body to another, our different bodies are so much alike that we don't realize our own transmigration.

or community, but for all, and friends as well as enemies are equally entitled to hear and benefit from it.

The Supreme Lord
"While speaking learned words, you are mourning for what is not worthy of grief. Those who are wise lament neither for the living nor the dead."

The Lord immediately takes the position of a teacher and speaks strongly, indirectly telling Arjuna that he's a fool. A learned person knows that the body will die eventually; therefore the body is not as important as the soul. One who knows this does not lament, regardless of the condition of the body.

"Never was there a time when I did not exist, nor you, nor all these kings; nor in the future shall any of us cease to be."

The Lord clearly says that He Himself, Arjuna, and all the fighters are eternally individual spiritual beings. They existed as spiritual individuals in the past, and they will remain eternal spiritual persons. Their individuality existed in the past and will continue in the future. Therefore, there is no cause for lamentation for anyone. The Lord then gives evidence of the soul's existence in the body and explains what happens to it after it leaves this body.

"As the embodied soul continuously passes, in this body, from childhood to youth to old age, the soul similarly passes into another body at death. A sober person is not bewildered by such a change. As a person puts on new

The soul does not age as the body does. The so-called old man may there-fore keep his youthful spirit although his body can't work as well as it did when young.

garments, giving up old ones, the soul similarly accepts new material bodies, giving up the old and useless ones."

Since every living entity is an individual soul, each is changing its body at every moment, manifesting sometimes as a child, sometimes as a youth, and sometimes as an old person. Yet the same spirit soul dwells within and does not undergo any change. At death this individual soul leaves the body and transmigrates to another body, just as one gives up

As winter comes and goes, so do happiness and distress. Krishna tells Arjuna to remain even-minded though perceiving such dualities. As a man must do his work in spite of bad weather, or a student must go to school even though he would rather not, Arjuna must fight because it's his duty as a soldier. He should not forsake his duty because of the temporary pains that arise in the course of its performance.

an old coat for a new one. One who knows about the soul, God, and material nature is called "sober" and is not deluded by bodily changes.

As long as one has a material body, one sometimes experiences happiness and at other times misery, much as one experiences alternating summer and winter seasons. Krishna advises Arjuna to tolerate these fluctuations without being disturbed, for one who does so is eligible for liberation. He then explains the nature of the soul.

Lord Krishna continues,
"Those who are seers of the truth have concluded that the material body does not endure and the soul does not change."

The body is changing at every moment by the action and reaction of the different cells, and thus growth and old age take place. But the spirit soul exists permanently, remaining despite all mental and bodily changes. By nature, the body—which is material—is ever-changing, and the soul—which is spiritual—is eternal.

Bodily changes don't affect the soul and, unlike the body, the soul never becomes old. (The so-called old person, therefore, feels himself to be in the same spirit as in his childhood or youth.) Neither does the soul have children; children are also individual souls who appear as the sons or daughters of particular parents.

The symptom of the soul's presence is consciousness. Each person is conscious of the pleasures and pains of his or her body, and therefore each body is the embodiment of an individual soul. This soul is a spiritual atom, smaller than the material atoms. Such atoms are innumerable and cannot be perceived by material instruments.

A spirit soul dwells in the heart of each living entity, and thus all the energies of bodily movement emanate from the heart. The corpuscles that carry oxygen from the lungs gather energy from the soul. When the soul passes away from this position, the activity of the blood, generating fusion, ceases. The material body minus consciousness is a dead body, and this consciousness cannot be revived in the body by any material means. Medical science accepts the importance of the red corpuscles, but it cannot ascertain that the source of the energy is the soul, although medical science does admit that the heart is the seat of all energies of the body.

By negation, Lord Krishna further defines the soul: "The soul pervades the entire body and is indestructible. No one is able to destroy the imperishable soul. For the soul there is neither birth nor death at any time. It has not come into being, does not come into being, and will not come into being. It is unborn, eternal, ever-existing, and primeval. It is not slain when the body is slain. The soul can never be cut to pieces by any weapon, nor burned by fire, nor moistened by water, nor withered by the wind. This individual soul is unbreakable and insoluble.

"If, however, you think that life symptoms are born and then die forever, you still have no reason to lament, O Arjuna."

For the sake of argument, Krishna presents an atheistic view: if the body is a combination of matter that developed life by chemical interaction, then why lament the loss of a certain bulk of chemicals? Analyzed in this way, the atheist, like the theist, has no reason to lament.

Then the Lord begins speaking of Arjuna's duty. Since Arjuna is a military man, the best engagement for him is to fight for religious principles; and so he need not hesitate. His duty is to protect the citizens from all kinds of difficulties, and for that reason he is obliged to apply violence in this case to maintain law and order. "If you do not perform your religious duty of fighting," Krishna says, "then you will certainly incur sins for neglecting your duties and thus lose your reputation as a fighter. People will always speak of your infamy, and for a respectable person, dishonor is worse than death. Your enemies will describe you in many unkind words and scorn your ability. What could be more painful for You?

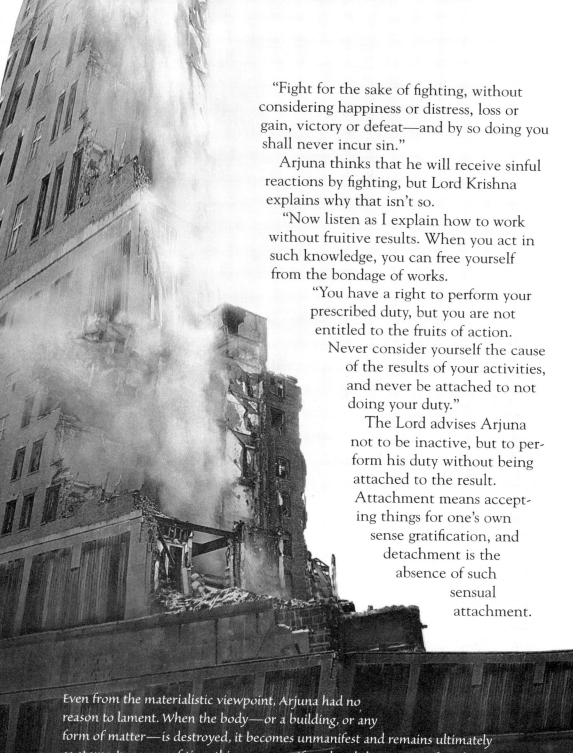

"Fight for the sake of fighting, without considering happiness or distress, loss or gain, victory or defeat—and by so doing you shall never incur sin."

Arjuna thinks that he will receive sinful reactions by fighting, but Lord Krishna explains why that isn't so.

"Now listen as I explain how to work without fruitive results. When you act in such knowledge, you can free yourself from the bondage of works.

"You have a right to perform your prescribed duty, but you are not entitled to the fruits of action. Never consider yourself the cause of the results of your activities, and never be attached to not doing your duty."

The Lord advises Arjuna not to be inactive, but to perform his duty without being attached to the result. Attachment means accepting things for one's own sense gratification, and detachment is the absence of such sensual attachment.

Even from the materialistic viewpoint, Arjuna had no reason to lament. When the body—or a building, or any form of matter—is destroyed, it becomes unmanifest and remains ultimately as atoms. In course of time things are manifested and then unmanifested, and in either stage nothing is lost. So what cause is there for lamentation?

But those fixed in Krishna consciousness have neither attachment nor detachment because their lives are dedicated to the service of the Lord. One who is attached to the result of one's work is also bound to the reaction: either enjoyment or suffering. Arjuna's nonparticipation in the battle is another side of attachment; and any attachment, positive or negative, is cause for bondage. Inaction is sinful. Therefore, fighting as a matter of duty is the only auspicious path for Arjuna.

"Perform your duty equipoised, O Arjuna, abandoning all attachment to success or failure. Such equanimity is called yoga."

Yoga means to concentrate the mind upon the Supreme Lord by controlling the ever-disturbing senses, and to follow His directions. In the highest sense, "yoga" means to link with the Supreme Lord by pleasing Him with loving devotional service.

"Persons engaged in devotional service rid themselves of both good and bad actions, even in this life. Therefore strive for yoga, which is the art of all work."

By engaging in devotional service to the Lord, great devotees have freed themselves from the results of work in the material world, and thus from the cycle of birth and death. Lord Krishna encourages Arjuna to follow their example and attain that state beyond all miseries, the spiritual kingdom. If he tries in this way, he will never be the loser.

"In this endeavor there is no loss or diminution, and a little advancement on this path can protect one from the most dangerous type of fear." In other words, unlike material activities and their results, which end with the body, God conscious activities have a permanent effect. If a person completes two percent in Krishna consciousness in this lifetime, the next beginning will be from three percent.

"Those who are on this path are resolute in purpose, and their aim is one. O Arjuna, the intelligence of those who are irresolute is many-branched." Those who are resolute have knowledge that God is the cause of all causes and all that be, and they have strong faith that by God consciousness they will be elevated to the highest perfection of life. On the other hand, those who are irresolute are attached to sense enjoyment and material opulence, and bewildered by such things, they do not desire to serve the Supreme Lord with devotion.

Arjuna
"O Krishna, what are the symptoms of one whose consciousness is thus merged in transcendence? How does such a person speak, sit, and walk?"

The Supreme Lord
"O Arjuna, when one gives up all desires for sense gratification, which arise from mental concoction, and when one's mind, thus purified, finds satisfaction in the self alone, one is in transcendental consciousness."

One who is able to withdraw one's senses from sense objects, as the tortoise draws its limbs within the shell, is firmly fixed in perfect consciousness.

As a strong wind sweeps away a boat on the water, even one of the roaming senses on which the mind focuses can carry away a person's intelligence.

Such persons speak only of Krishna and of matters relating to Him. They are not disturbed amidst distress or failure, nor elated by happiness or success. God conscious persons are steady in their determination.

Though one may be restricted from sense enjoyment, one's taste for sense objects remains. But by experiencing a higher taste, the taste of serving the Lord with love, one stops seeking sense enjoyment and becomes fixed in God consciousness. On the path of God consciousness, however, there may be obstacles.

"The senses are so strong and impetuous, O Arjuna, that they forcibly carry away the mind even of a person of discrimination who is endeavoring to control them."

By contemplating sense objects, one develops attachment for them, and from such attachment lust develops, and when lust is unfulfilled, anger follows.

But those who are free from attachment and aversion, who control the senses and fix their consciousness upon the Lord, can receive His mercy. One who is not connected with the Supreme, however, can have neither transcendental intelligence nor a steady mind, without which there is no possibility of peace. "And," Krishna asks Arjuna, "how can there be any happiness without peace?"

It's not that the Lord expects Arjuna to become free of material demands—as long as one has a material body, the demands of the body for sense gratification will continue. But He does expect Arjuna to be undisturbed by material desires, for even one of the senses engaged in the desire for material pleasure can create a disturbance.

The Supreme Lord concludes,

"A person who is not disturbed by the incessant flow of desires—that enter like rivers into the ocean, which is ever being filled but is always still—can alone achieve peace, and not the person who strives to satisfy such desires.

"That is the way of spiritual and godly life, after which attained, a person is not bewildered. If one is thus situated, even at the hour of death, one can enter into the kingdom of God."

Desires are compared to rivers, and the ocean is compared to a saintly person's mind. Although many turbulent rivers fill the ocean with their waters, the ocean remains undisturbed. Similarly, although desires may come upon saintly persons, such persons are not disturbed, for they are full in themselves. Thus they remain peaceful.

Artificial renouncers—so-called swamis—are actually pretenders who simply think of sense gratification. Better to remain in one's position, Krishna says, carry out one's duties without attachment, and make gradual spiritual progress. A sincere person who follows this method is far better situated than the pretender who adopts showy spiritualism to cheat the innocent public. Clearly the Lord doesn't want Arjuna to give up his duty as a military general and become a pseudo-spiritualist, living at the expense of others.

3

Karma-yoga

RJUNA IS CONFUSED. Krishna has told him to control his senses and become detached, perhaps indicating that Krishna consciousness means inaction. Yet the Lord also said that Arjuna should fight. As a sincere student, Arjuna asks for clarification.

Arjuna
"O Krishna, why do You want to engage me in this ghastly warfare, if You think that intelligence is better than fruitive work?"

The Supreme Lord
"O sinless Arjuna, two classes of people try to realize the self. Some are inclined to understand it by philosophical speculation, and others by devotional service."

In other words, some seekers of the Truth analyze matter and spirit, whereas others work in Krishna consciousness. However, the two methods are interdependent, as are philosophy and religion. Philosophy without religion is mental speculation, while religion without philosophy is sentiment, or sometimes fanaticism. Ultimately, the aim of both the analytical and active processes is to understand the soul in relation to God.

Because the soul is always active, our body is active; without the soul's presence, the body is inert matter. Krishna tells Arjuna to act according to the nature of his body—not to renounce activity artificially.

One cannot even maintain one's physical body without work. But work done for sense gratification has a reaction, either good or bad, and any reaction binds the performer. "Therefore, O Arjuna," Krishna says,

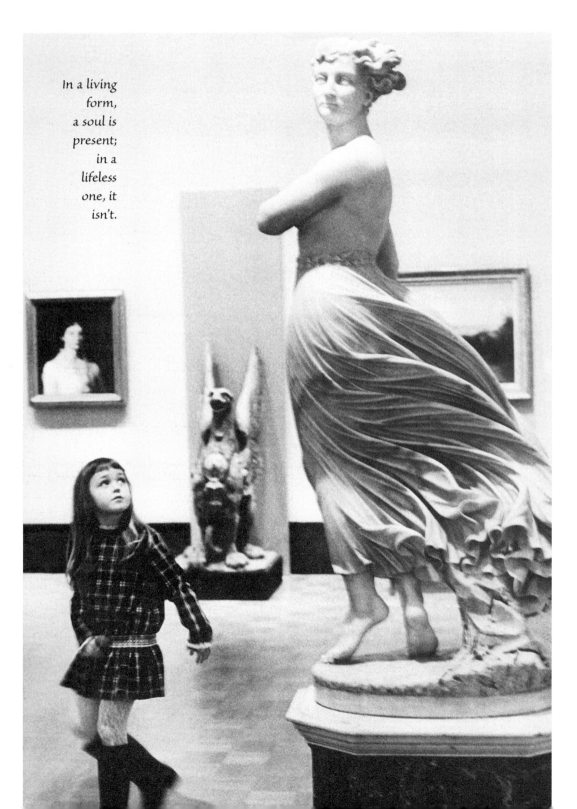

In a living
form,
a soul is
present;
in a
lifeless
one, it
isn't.

All the necessities of life—food, water, air, light—are supplied not by factories but by material nature which works under the direction of the Supreme Lord. If there's no rain, then despite all our technological advancement, crops die.

"perform your prescribed duties for My satisfaction, and in that way always remain free from bondage." This practice will save one from the reaction of work and gradually elevate one to transcendental loving service of the Lord, which alone can take one to God's kingdom.

One who's qualified to enter God's kingdom, who is fully Krishna conscious, no longer has any duty to perform. Such a person isn't interested in material activities and does not take pleasure in material arrangements. "Those who are self-realized have no purpose to fulfill in the discharge of their prescribed duties," Krishna says, "nor do they have any reason not to perform such work. Nor have they any need to depend on any other living being."

To attain this exalted stage, Arjuna should act as a matter of duty, without being attached to the fruits of his activities; he should fight in the battle for the interest of Krishna because Krishna wants him to fight. Arjuna's idea to be a good or nonviolent man is a personal attachment, but for him to act on behalf of the Supreme is to act without attachment to the result. That is perfect action, recommended by the Supreme Lord Krishna, and it is transcendental to all reactions.

"Whatever action a great person performs, common people follow. And whatever standards that person sets by exemplary acts, all the world pursues."

The cashier counts millions of dollars for her employer but claims not a cent for herself. Similarly, one who sees everything in relation to God realizes that everything belongs to Him.

Lord Krishna and Arjuna, the Lord's eternal friend, have no need to fight in the Battle of Kurukshetra, but they will fight to teach people in general that violence is also necessary in a situation where good arguments fail. Before the battle, every effort was made to avoid the war, even by the Supreme Lord Himself, but the other party was determined to fight. So for such a just cause, fighting is necessary. Although those who are Krishna conscious may not have any interest in the world, they still work to teach people how to act and live.

Krishna, God Himself, has no prescribed work. Nor is He in need of anything, nor does He have a need to obtain anything—and yet He still engages in prescribed duties, for if He ever failed to do so, people would follow His example and havoc would result.

"As the ignorant perform their duties with attachment to results, the learned person may similarly act, but without attachment, for the sake of leading people on the right path.

"One who is learned, who is in knowledge of the Absolute Truth, O Arjuna, does not engage himself in the senses and sense gratification, knowing well the differences between work in devotion and work for fruitive results. Therefore, O Arjuna, surrendering all your works unto Me, with full knowledge of Me, without desires for profit, with no claims to proprietorship, and free from lethargy, fight."

Krishna has several times asked Arjuna to be dutiful and detached, but here for the first time He asks Arjuna to fight with devotion. He then describes the result of acting in this way.

"Persons who execute their duties according to My injunctions and who follow this teaching faithfully, without envy, become free from the bondage of fruitive actions. But those who, out of envy, disregard these teachings and do not follow them are bereft of all knowledge, befooled, and ruined in their endeavors for perfection."

The simple qualification of firm faith in the eternal injunctions of the Lord, even by a beginner who's unable to execute such injunctions, qualifies one to become liberated from karma. In the beginning of Krishna consciousness, one may not fully discharge the injunctions of the Lord, but because one is not resentful of this principle and works sincerely, without consideration of defeat and hopelessness, one will surely be promoted to the stage of pure Krishna consciousness. Krishna doesn't want Arjuna to give up his duties abruptly, but to remain in his position and try to become God conscious. In this way he will gradually become detached from all kinds of sensual activities.

Arjuna
"O Krishna, by what is one impelled to sinful acts, even unwillingly, as if engaged by force?" We, as part and parcel of the Supreme, are originally spiritual, pure, and free from all material contaminations. But when in contact with the material nature, we act in many sinful ways without hesitation, and sometimes even against our will.

The Supreme Lord

"It is lust only, Arjuna, which is born of contact with the material mode of passion and later transformed into wrath, and which is the all-devouring sinful enemy of this world. The wise living entity's pure consciousness becomes covered by its eternal enemy in the form of lust, which is never satisfied and which burns like fire." When living entities come in contact with the material creation, their eternal love for Krishna is transformed into lust. When lust is unsatisfied, it turns into wrath; wrath is transformed into illusion, and illusion continues the material existence. Therefore, lust is the greatest enemy of the living entity, and it is lust only that induces the pure living entity to remain entangled in this material world.

"The senses, mind, and intelligence are the sitting places of this lust. Through these, lust covers the real knowledge of the living entities and bewilders them. Therefore, in the very beginning curb this great symbol of sin, lust, by regulating the senses, and slay this destroyer of knowledge and self-realization." When love of God deteriorates into lust, it's very difficult to return to the normal, God conscious condition; but it is possible by devotional service to the Supreme Lord, in which the soul is directly engaged with the Supreme. Then the soul's subordinates—the intelligence, mind, and senses—will be similarly engaged.

"The working senses are superior to dull matter, mind is higher than the senses, intelligence is still higher than the mind, and the soul is even higher than the intelligence. Thus knowing oneself to be transcendental to the material senses, mind, and intelligence, O mighty-armed Arjuna, one should steady the mind by deliberate spiritual intelligence and thus—by spiritual strength—conquer this insatiable enemy known as lust." If lust is transformed into love for the Supreme, or transformed into Krishna consciousness—in other words, desiring everything for Krishna—then lust can be spiritualized and thus conquered.

In summary, Arjuna's desire for sense gratification is his greatest enemy, but by dedicating his work to Krishna (*karma-yoga*), he could control his senses, mind, and intelligence and thus gradually become transcendentally situated.

As one who breaks the law is imprisoned, the soul covered by lust is imprisoned in the material world.

26

Ignorance is
compared to a
dangerous body
of water, and
transcendental
knowledge to
the boat that
can safely carry
one across it.

4

Transcendental Knowledge

AFTER RECOMMENDING KARMA-YOGA (non-fruitive action), Krishna explains how this yoga culminates in transcendental knowledge—knowledge concerning God, the soul, and their eternal relationship.

Krishna first mentions the history of the oral transmission of the *Gita* (originating with Himself) through disciplic succession.

The Supreme Lord
"I instructed this imperishable science of yoga to the sun-god, Vivasvan, and Vivasvan instructed it to Manu, the father of mankind, and Manu in turn instructed it to Iksvaku. This supreme science was thus received through the chain of disciplic succession, and the saintly kings understood it in that way. But in course of time the succession was broken, and therefore the science as it is appears to be lost."

When unscrupulous commentators interpret the *Gita* to accommodate their own interests, they distort the original purpose of this great text and cover its eternal truths. Krishna is speaking it again to reestablish those truths.

"That very ancient science of the relationship with the Supreme is today told by Me to you because you are My devotee as well as My friend and can therefore understand the transcendental mystery of this science."

After assuring Arjuna that he is qualified to receive this knowledge, Krishna explains His transcendental nature as the Supreme Lord and the reason for His periodic descents to the material world.

Lord Krishna manifested Himself as Lord Buddha (below), and also as Lord Chaitanya (right). As Lord Chaitanya He propagated a sublime and easy method of God realization especially suited for this age of quarrel, namely the chanting of the Lord's holy names: Hare Krishna, Hare Krishna, Krishna Krishna Hare Hare/Hare Rama, Hare Rama, Rama Rama, Hare Hare.

"Although I am unborn and My transcendental body never deteriorates, and although I am the Lord of all living entities, I still appear in every millennium in My original transcendental form."

The Lord's appearance and disappearance is like the sun's rising, moving before us, and then disappearing from our sight. When the sun is out of sight, we think that the sun is set, and when the sun is before our eyes, we think that the sun is on the horizon. Actually, the sun is always in its fixed position, but owing to our defective, insufficient senses, we calculate the appearance and disappearance of the sun.

Unlike the living entities in the material world, the Lord does not transmigrate from one body to another. Whenever He appears, He does so in the same original spiritual body, which never grows old or deteriorates. The Lord is conscious of all His

As a teacher instructs a student, one who is mature in spiritual realization teaches a neophyte. In this way—from a qualified spiritual teacher to a qualified spiritual student—the science of God consciousness has been passed down through the ages .

previous appearances and disappearances, while the living entities forget everything about their past body as soon as they enter another body.

"Whenever and wherever there is a decline in religious practice, O Arjuna, and a predominant rise of irreligion—at that time I descend Myself. To deliver the pious and to annihilate the miscreants, as well as to reestablish the principles of religion, I Myself appear, millennium after millennium." Although there are many transcendental forms of the Lord, they are still the same Supreme Person. Each incarnation of the Lord has a particular mission, which is described in the revealed scriptures. No one should be accepted as an incarnation unless the scriptures refer to him. The Lord's mission is always the same: to lead people to God consciousness and obedience to the principles of religion. Sometimes He descends personally, and sometimes He sends His bona fide representative in the form of His son, or servant, or Himself in some disguised form.

"Those who know the transcendental nature of My appearance and activities do not, upon leaving the body, take their birth again in this material world, but attain My eternal abode, O Arjuna.

"Being freed from attachment, fear and anger, being fully absorbed in Me and taking refuge in Me, many, many persons in the past became purified by knowledge of Me—and thus they all attained transcendental love for Me." Some people are too materially attached and therefore do not give attention to spiritual life, some are fearful of spiritual individuality and personality and want to merge into the supreme spirit, and some disbelieve in everything, being angry at all sorts of spiritual speculation out of hopelessness. For success in spiritual life, one must rid oneself of attachment to, fear of, and anger about the material world by the process of devotional service.

"As all surrender unto Me, I reward them accordingly. Everyone follows My path in all respects, O Arjuna." Everyone is dependent for success upon God's mercy alone, and all kinds of spiritual processes are but different degrees of success on the same path. Whether one is without material desires, or full of material desires, or seeks liberation, one should with all effort worship the Supreme Lord for complete perfection, culminating in God consciousness.

Most people, however, have little interest in spiritual knowledge. Rather, they work hard for material enjoyment through the pursuit of wealth, power, and prestige. Recognizing these prevalent tendencies, Lord Krishna created a social system so that everyone, while working according to their propensity, could also make steady spiritual advancement.

Lord Krishna continues,
"According to the three modes of material nature and the work associated with them, the four divisions of human society are created by Me.

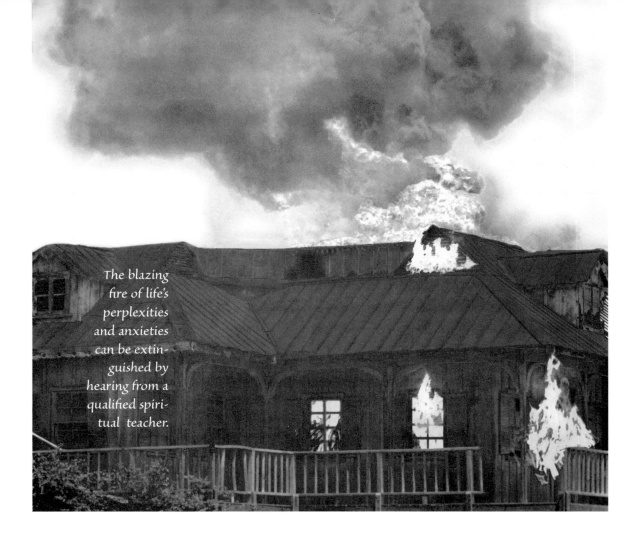

The blazing fire of life's perplexities and anxieties can be extinguished by hearing from a qualified spiritual teacher.

And although I am the creator of this system, you should know that I am yet the nondoer, being unchangeable."

The three modes of material nature are goodness, passion, and ignorance, and Krishna elaborates on them in Chapter Fourteen. The four divisions of society are: the learned and pious teachers, the military fighters and governmental administrators, the farmers and merchants, and the laborers. The Lord will further describe these in Chapter Eighteen. In spite of His creating these four divisions, Krishna does not belong to any of them because He is not a conditioned soul.

All conditioned souls are subject to the reactions of their past good or bad activities; the Lord provides the facilities for such activities, but He is not responsible for the activities that we perform. We are responsible for our own acts. As He says, "There is no work that affects Me."

Nor does the Lord "aspire for the fruits of action." One who thinks that the Supreme Person desires fruitive results certainly becomes entangled in fruitive reactions, but one who understands the transcendental nature of the Lord is not subject to the laws of karma. "All the liberated souls in ancient times acted with this understanding of My transcendental nature. Therefore you should perform your duty, following in their footsteps."

Krishna explains that those who are Krishna conscious are free from the bonds of karma. They act for Krishna; therefore they do not enjoy or suffer any of the effects of their work. This is called "akarma" or inaction in action (because there is no reaction to any action), and those who act in this way, without desire for personal sense gratification, are in full knowledge and enjoy transcendental happiness.

Abandoning all attachment to the results of their activities, ever satisfied and independent, such devotees of the Lord perform no fruitive action, although engaged in all kinds of undertakings. They have realized their constitutional position as eternal servitors of the Supreme Lord and act out of pure love for Him. Therefore they have no attraction for the results of their action. They do their duty to the best of their ability and leave everything to Krishna.

Krishna conscious persons neither beg nor borrow, but labor honestly as far as is within their power, and are satisfied with whatever they obtain by their own honest labor. Since they want only to satisfy the Supreme Lord with their work, they are happy and steady both in success and failure.

"Just try to learn the truth by approaching a spiritual master," Lord Krishna says. "Inquire submissively and render service unto such a person. The self-realized souls can impart knowledge unto you because they have seen the truth."

No one can be spiritually realized by manufacturing a process; mental speculation and dry arguments cannot lead one to the right path. Nor by independent study of books of knowledge can one progress in spiritual life. One must approach a bona fide spiritual master in the line of disciplic succession from the Lord Himself, and accept and serve such a highly qualified spiritual master without false prestige. Satisfaction of the self-realized spiritual master is the secret of advancement in spiritual life.

"Having obtained real knowledge from a self-realized soul, you will never fall again into such illusion, for by this knowledge you will see that all living beings are but part of the Supreme, or in other words, that they are Mine." Arjuna, under illusion, thought that the temporary bodily relationship with his kinsmen was more important than his eternal spiritual relationship with Krishna, but in reality his kinsmen are Krishna's eternal servitors, as is Arjuna himself. Having forgotten his eternal service, Arjuna is perplexed by the material energy.

"Even if you are considered to be the most sinful of all sinners, when you are situated in the boat of transcendental knowledge you will be able to cross over the ocean of miseries." In the ocean, however expert a swimmer one may be, the struggle for existence is severe. If someone

The science of self-realization is the boat that
enables one to cross the ocean of miseries.

comes and lifts the struggling swimmer from the ocean, that person is the greatest savior.

"As blazing fire turns firewood to ashes, O Arjuna, so does the fire of knowledge burn to ashes all reactions to material activities. In this world, there is nothing so sublime and pure as transcendental knowledge. Such knowledge is the mature fruit of all mysticism. And those who have become accomplished in the practice of devotional service enjoy this knowledge within themselves in due course of time." Ignorance causes bondage, and knowledge causes liberation. This knowledge is the mature fruit of devotional service, and those situated in transcendental knowledge need not search for peace elsewhere, for they enjoy peace within themselves.

"Faithful persons who are dedicated to transcendental knowledge and who subdue their senses are eligible to achieve such knowledge, and having achieved it they quickly attain the supreme spiritual peace. But ignorant and faithless persons who doubt the revealed scriptures do not attain God consciousness; they fall down. For the doubting soul there is happiness neither in this world nor in the next.

Even in ordinary deal-
ings, faith is required—
you must have faith that
the barber won't slit
your throat with his
blade. Similarly, in
spiritual life, faith in the
bona fide teachers and
scriptures is required.

"One who acts in devotional service, renouncing the fruits of those actions, and whose doubts have been destroyed by transcendental knowledge, is situated factually in the self. Such a person is not bound by the reactions of work, O Arjuna.

"Therefore the doubts which have arisen in your heart out of ignorance should be slashed by the weapon of knowledge. Armed with yoga, O Arjuna, stand and fight."

A person situated in the self sees that the soul within, not the body, is the attractive, joyful, loving force. When the soul leaves the body (at death), the body is no longer attractive.

5

Action in Krishna Consciousness

IN CHAPTER THREE, KRISHNA SAYS that one who is self-realized has no duties. Yet at the end of Chapter Four, Krishna tells Arjuna to arm himself with yoga and fight. Arjuna wonders if he should be inactive in knowledge or active in devotion.

Arjuna
"O Krishna, first of all You ask me to renounce work, and then again You recommend work with devotion. Now will You kindly tell me definitely which of the two is more beneficial?"

The Supreme Lord
"The renunciation of work and work in devotion are both good for liberation. But, of the two, work in devotional service is better than renunciation of work." Renunciation is complete when done with the knowledge that everything in existence belongs to the Lord. One should understand that, factually, since nothing belongs to anyone, then where is the question of proprietorship or of renunciation? One who knows that everything is Krishna's property is always situated in renunciation. Since everything belongs to Krishna, we should employ everything in His service.

There is no difference between the conclusions reached by an analytical study of the material world, in which one becomes detached

When from a distance we watch a person fly a kite, we can't always tell if she's letting the kite go higher or bringing it down. Nor from what people are doing can we always tell if they are becoming free from karma or taking on more.

from matter, and devotional service, in which one becomes attached to Krishna. Detachment from matter and attachment to Krishna are the same. "One who knows that the position reached by means of analytical study can also be attained by devotional service, and who therefore sees analytical study and devotional service to be on the same level, sees things as they are.

"Merely renouncing all activities yet not engaging in the devotional service of the Lord cannot make one happy. But a thoughtful person engaged in devotional service can achieve the Supreme without delay.

"Those who work in devotion, who are pure souls, who control their mind and senses, are dear to everyone, and everyone is dear to them. Though always working, they are never entangled." Because those who work in Krishna consciousness are servants to all, they are dear to everyone. And because everyone is satisfied with their work, they are pure in consciousness.

"Those who perform their duty without attachment, surrendering the results unto the Supreme Lord, are unaffected by sinful action, as lotus leaves are untouched by water." Even our material body, being a gift of the Lord for carrying out a particular type of action, can be engaged in Krishna consciousness. Then our body becomes uncontaminated by sinful reactions, exactly as the lotus leaf, though in a pond, is not wet.

The difference between God conscious and bodily conscious people is that the former are attached to God, whereas the latter are attached to the results of their activities and use those results for sensual pleasures. People who are attached to God and work only for Him are liberated and have no anxiety over the results of their work. "The steadily devoted souls attain unadulterated peace because they offer the result of all activities to Me; whereas persons who are not in union with the Divine, who are greedy for the fruits of their labor, become entangled."

The living entity's temporary body or material dwelling place causes varieties of activities and their resultant reactions. In such a conditional atmosphere, one suffers the results of the activities of the body by identifying (in ignorance) with the body. Ignorance, acquired from time immemorial, is the cause of bodily suffering and distress. As soon as one

A wise person is in the world but not of it, as the lotus leaf is in the water but not wet.

becomes aloof from the activities of the body, one becomes free from the reactions as well. The Supreme Lord does not create the living entity's particular situation, but the living entity, bewildered by bodily identification, desires certain conditions of life, and thereby the chain of action and reaction begins.

When we are bewildered by material desires, the Lord allows us to fulfill those desires, but the Lord is never responsible for the actions and reactions that result from those desires. The Lord can fulfill all desires, but, being neutral to everyone, He does not interfere with our desires. However, when we desire Him, the Lord takes special care and encourages us to desire in such a way that we can attain Him and be eternally happy.

"When one is enlightened with the knowledge by which ignorance is destroyed, then one's knowledge reveals everything, as the sun lights up everything in the daytime."

An enlightened person distinguishes neither between species nor castes. In Krishna's words, "The humble sages, by virtue of true knowledge, see with equal vision a learned and gentle *brahmana*, a cow, an elephant, a dog, and a dog-eater." The *brahmana* (learned, pious teacher) and the dog-eater may differ from the social point of view, or a dog, a cow, and an elephant may differ from the point of view of species, but these bodily distinctions are meaningless from the transcendentalist's viewpoint. This equanimity of vision is the sign of self-realization. As

Within each living thing a soul resides, equal in quality to all others. Spiritually, all living beings are equal.

45

the Lord is flawless, being free from attraction or hatred, so when living entities relinquish attraction or hatred, they also become flawless and eligible to enter God's kingdom. Such persons know perfectly well that they are not their bodies, but fragmental portions of the Supreme Lord. Many transcendental symptoms result from this realization.

"A person who neither rejoices upon achieving something pleasant nor laments upon obtaining something unpleasant, who is self-intelligent, who is unbewildered, and who knows the science of God, is already situated in transcendence. Such a liberated person is not attracted to material sense pleasure but is always in trance, enjoying the pleasure within. In this way the self-realized person enjoys unlimited happiness by concentrating on the Supreme." Those in Krishna consciousness are so happy in the loving service of the Lord that the taste for material sense pleasure vanishes altogether.

"An intelligent person does not take part in the sources of misery, which are due to contact with the material senses. O Arjuna, such pleasures have a beginning and an end, and so the wise person does not delight in them."

Those who are true yogis or learned transcendentalists are not attracted by sense pleasure, which is the cause of continuous material existence.

"Before giving up this present body, if one is able to tolerate the urges of the material senses and check the force of desire and anger, one is well situated and is happy in this world. One whose happiness is within, who is active and rejoices within, and whose aim is inward is actually the perfect

When friends wear costumes, they are unrecognizable. Similarly, every soul in this world is dressed with a material body and cannot be recognized by material vision.

46

mystic. Such a person is liberated by experiencing the Supreme within, and thereby ultimately attains the Supreme."

In Krishna's view, welfare work does not mean only ministering to the physical welfare of human society. Temporary relief for the body is incomplete. The cause of difficulties in life is forgetfulness of our relationship with the Supreme Lord. So true welfare work must also include reviving our God consciousness and the God consciousness within other living beings.

"A person in full consciousness of Me, knowing Me as the ultimate enjoyer of all sacrifices and austerities, the Supreme Lord of all planets and demigods, and the benefactor and well-wisher of all living entities, attains peace from the pangs of material miseries." People are anxious about attaining peace in the material world. But they do not know the formula for peace, which Krishna explains in this part of the *Bhagavad-gita*. The greatest peace formula is simply this: whatever work we do is meant to be offered unto God. We should do everything for and offer everything to the transcendental service of the Lord because He is the proprietor of everything. No one is greater than He, and He is the greatest friend of each living being.

Under the spell of illusion, living entities are trying to be lords of the material energy, but actually they are dominated by it. Krishna is the master of material nature, and the conditioned souls are under the stringent rules of material nature. Those who understand these facts will achieve peace in the world, individually and collectively. Krishna consciousness brings one into spiritual life even while one is within the jurisdiction of matter, for its practice arouses spiritual existence in the material world. And it can award peace to the human being.

A carpenter cannot rightly claim that his creations are his; they belong to his employer. In the same way, whatever we have and whatever we create belong to God, for He has provided all the natural resources we utilize, as well as our ability and intelligence to utilize them.

6

The Yoga of Meditation

IN THIS CHAPTER THE LORD EXPLAINS a process of yoga for controlling the mind and senses, and He explains that the perfect yogi is the person who acts for the satisfaction of the Supreme.

The Supreme Lord
"Those who are unattached to the fruits of their work and who work as they are obligated are in the renounced order of life and are the true mystics, not those who light no fire and perform no duty. What is called renunciation you should know to be the same as yoga, or linking oneself with the Supreme, O Arjuna, for one can never become a yogi unless one renounces the desire for sense gratification.

"A person is said to be elevated in yoga when, having renounced all material desires, that person neither acts for sense gratification nor engages in fruitive activities.

"We must deliver ourselves with the help of our minds, and not degrade ourselves. The mind is the friend of the conditioned soul, and the enemy as well. For one who has conquered the mind, the mind is the best of friends; but for one who has failed to do so, the mind will remain the greatest enemy."

One who cannot control the mind lives always with the greatest enemy, and thus one's life and its mission are spoiled. As long as the mind remains an unconquered enemy, one has to serve the dictates of

A wild, unbridled horse is like an uncontrolled mind—
unpredictable, disturbing, and dangerous. In this chapter
Krishna explains the importance of conquering the mind, gives
the means for doing so, and speaks of the resulting self-mastery.

lust, greed, hatred, envy, and anger. But when the mind is conquered, one voluntarily agrees to abide by the dictations of the Supreme Lord, who is situated within everyone's heart as the Supersoul. "For those who have conquered the mind, the Supersoul is already reached, for they are tranquil. To such people, happiness and distress, heat and cold, honor and dishonor are all the same.

"One is said to be established in self-realization and is called a yogi when one is fully satisfied by virtue of acquired knowledge and realization. Such a person is situated in transcendence, is self-controlled, and sees everything—whether it be pebbles, stones, or gold—as the same.

"One is considered still further advanced when one regards honest well-wishers, affectionate benefactors, the neutral, mediators, the envious, friends and enemies, the pious and the sinners all with an equal mind.

"A transcendentalist should always engage the body, mind, and self in relationship with the Supreme, should live alone in a secluded place, should always carefully control the mind, and should be free from desires and feelings of possessiveness."

The first business of transcendentalists is to keep their minds always on Krishna. They should always think of Krishna and not forget Him even for a moment. Such persons know that everything belongs to Krishna, and thus they are free from feelings of personal possession. They know how to accept things favorable to Krishna consciousness and how to reject things unfavorable to Krishna consciousness.

Out of many good medicines, a doctor prescribes the one that's right for us. Similarly, out of many bona fide ways of self-realization— one being the mystic yoga process mentioned above—Krishna prescribes the way that's best for us. He's the expert doctor and at the end of this chapter He gives us His personal advice.

"To practice yoga, one should go to a secluded place and should lay kusa grass on the ground and then cover it with a deerskin and a soft cloth. The seat should be neither too high nor too low and should be situated in a sacred place. The yogi should then sit on it firmly and practice yoga to purify the heart by controlling the mind, senses, and activities, and fixing the mind on one point. One should hold one's body, neck, and head erect in a straight line and stare steadily at the tip of the nose. Thus, with an unagitated, subdued mind, devoid of fear, completely free from sex life, one should meditate upon Me within the heart and make Me the ultimate goal of life." This process of spiritual realization, suitable for previous ages, is often not possible to follow in this age of quarrel and hypocrisy. As the Lord will later explain, we can attain the same goal by the process of *bhakti-yoga*.

"Thus practicing constant control of the body, mind, and activities, the mystic transcendentalist, with mind regulated, attains the kingdom of God by cessation of material existence." Yoga practice is not meant for attaining material facility; it is to enable the cessation of material existence and entrance into the spiritual sky, the abode of the Lord.

"There is no possibility of one's becoming a yogi, O Arjuna, if one eats too much or eats too little, sleeps too much or does not sleep enough. One who is regulated in the habits of eating, sleeping, recreation, and work can mitigate all material pains by practicing the yoga system.

"When one, by practice of yoga, disciplines the mental activities and becomes situated in transcendence—devoid of all material desires—one is said to be well established in yoga.

"In the stage of perfection called trance, or *samadhi*, one's mind is completely restrained from material mental

As a flame in a windless place does not waver, so the transcendentalist, whose mind is controlled, remains always steady in meditation on the transcendent Self.

activities by practice of yoga. This perfection is characterized by one's ability to see the soul and the Supersoul (God in the heart) by the pure mind and to relish and rejoice in the Supersoul. In that joyous state, one is situated in boundless transcendental happiness, realized through transcendental senses. Thus established, one never departs from the truth, and upon gaining this position one thinks there is no greater gain. Being thus situated, one is never shaken, even in the midst of greatest difficulty. This indeed is actual freedom from all miseries arising from material contact.

"One should engage oneself in the practice of yoga with determination and faith and not be deviated from the path. One should abandon, without exception, all material desires born of mental speculation and thus control all the senses by the mind. Gradually, step by step, one becomes situated in trance by means of intelligence sustained by full conviction, and thus the mind is fixed on the Supersoul alone and thinks of nothing else. From wherever the mind wanders due to its flickering and unsteady nature, one must certainly withdraw it and bring it back under the control of the self.

"The yogi whose mind is fixed on Me verily attains the highest transcendental happiness. That person is beyond the mode of passion, realizes his qualitative identity with the Supreme, and is thus freed from all reactions to past deeds. The self-controlled yogi, constantly engaged in yoga practice, becomes free from all material contamination and achieves happiness in transcendental loving service to the Lord.

"A true yogi observes Me in all beings and also sees every being in Me. Indeed, the self-realized person sees Me everywhere." Yogis see everyone equally because they see that all living entities, although in different situations according to the results of their work, in all circumstances remain servants of God. While in the material energy, one serves the material senses, and while in the spiritual energy, one serves the Supreme Lord directly. The yogi knows that everything is a manifestation of Krishna's energy, that nothing can exist without Krishna, and that Krishna is the Lord of everything.

"For one who sees Me everywhere and sees everything in Me, I am never lost, nor is that person ever lost to Me. Such a yogi, who engages in the worshipful service of the Supersoul, knowing that I and the Supersoul are one, remains always in Me in all circumstances." Krishna in the form of Supersoul is situated in everyone's heart. There is no difference between the innumerable Supersouls present in the innumerable hearts of living entities. In this way, Krishna is one, and yet, He is all-pervading. By His inconceivable potency, in spite of His one form, He is present everywhere, as the sun appears in many places at once.

"The perfect yogis are those who, by comparison to their own selves, see the true equality of all beings, in times of both happiness and distress, O Arjuna!" Those who are Krishna conscious are perfect yogis; they are aware of everyone's happiness and distress by dint of their personal experience. The cause of distress is forgetfulness of one's relationship with God. And the cause of happiness is knowing Krishna to be the supreme enjoyer of the activities of human beings, the proprietor of all lands and planets, and the most dear friend of all living entities.

Arjuna
"O Krishna, the system of yoga which You have summarized appears impractical and unendurable to me, for the mind is restless, unsteady, turbulent, obstinate, and very strong, O Krishna, and to subdue it, I think, is more difficult than controlling the wind." Arjuna rejects as impractical

Like the mind, water is easily
disturbed. But when water is
sheltered it gradually becomes
calm, like the mind that follows
the regulations of yoga.

the system of mysticism described by Lord Krishna. In this age most people cannot leave home for a secluded place in the mountains or jungle to practice yoga. People are not concerned about self-realization even by simple means, what to speak of such a difficult yoga system. As a practical man, Arjuna thought it impossible to practice this system of yoga, even though he belonged to the royal family, was an accomplished fighter, had great longevity, and, above all, was the most intimate friend of Lord Krishna, the Supreme Person. Therefore, if impossible for Arjuna, how could this system apply to the ordinary person?

Lord Krishna
"O mighty-armed one, it is undoubtedly very difficult to curb the restless mind, but it is possible by suitable practice and by detachment." The foremost "suitable practice" is to hear about God. The more one hears about God, the more one becomes enlightened and detached from everything that draws the mind away from God. "Hearing" includes not only learning from self-realized souls, but also studying and contemplating God's words in authorized scriptures like the *Bhagavad-gita*. Thus reading the *Bhagavad-gita* is also a "suitable practice."

"For one whose mind is unbridled, self-realization is difficult work. But one whose mind is controlled and who strives by appropriate means is assured of success. That is My opinion." Trying to practice yoga while engaging the mind in material enjoyment is like trying to ignite a fire while pouring water on it. Yoga practice without mental control is a waste of time. Such a show of yoga may be materially lucrative, but it is useless as far as spiritual realization is concerned.

Arjuna
"O Krishna, what is the destination of the unsuccessful transcendentalist, who in the beginning takes to the process of self-realization with faith, but who later desists due to worldly-mindedness and thus does not attain perfection in mysticism?

Arjuna compares the churning, strong, obstinate mind to the wind. As the wind cannot be stopped, neither can the mind. But Krishna explains that by suitable practice—hearing about the Lord—and by detachment from material life, the mind can be controlled.

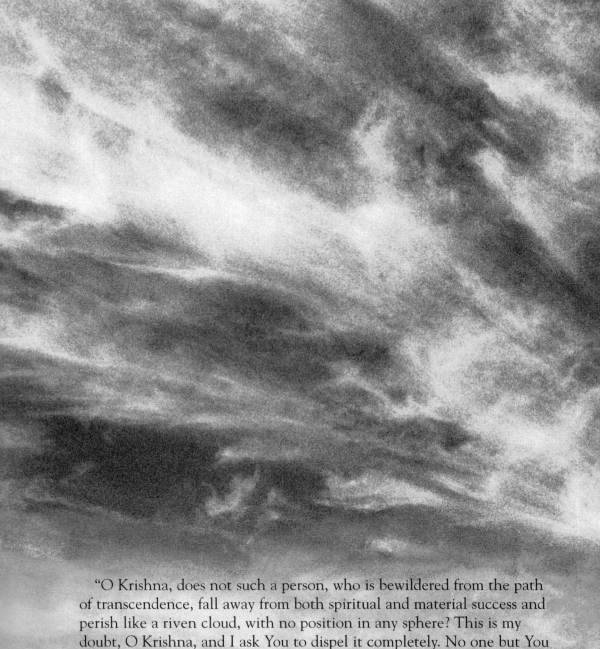

"O Krishna, does not such a person, who is bewildered from the path of transcendence, fall away from both spiritual and material success and perish like a riven cloud, with no position in any sphere? This is my doubt, O Krishna, and I ask You to dispel it completely. No one but You can destroy this doubt." Despite endeavoring for self-realization, one may fail if one is not sufficiently serious about following the process. To pursue the transcendental path is an attempt to escape the clutches of material vision—to declare war against it. So the material energy tries

Arjuna asks,
"What happens
to a person
who gives up
material life to
be a spiritualist
but fails? Is that
person like a
cloud torn
asunder, with
no position in
either world?"

to defeat the practitioner by various allurements. A conditioned soul identifies itself with the material body and so is already allured by the material energy. And there is every chance of it being allured again, even while performing transcendental disciplines.

The Supreme Lord
"Arjuna, a transcendentalist engaged in auspicious activities does not meet with destruction either in this world or in the spiritual world; one

who does good, My friend, is never overcome by evil. Yogis who are unsuccessful after short practice of yoga enjoy many years on higher planets (where pious living entities reside), and then are reborn on this planet into a family of righteous people, or a family of rich aristocracy. However, if unsuccessful after long practice of yoga, they take birth in a family of transcendentalists who are surely great in wisdom. Certainly, such a birth is rare in this world.

"On taking such a birth, those persons revive the divine consciousness of their previous lives, and again try to make further progress in order to achieve complete success. By virtue of their divine consciousness of the previous life, they automatically become attracted to the yogic principles—even without seeking them. Such inquisitive transcendentalists stand always above the ritualistic principles of the scriptures. And when a yogi engages with sincere endeavor in making further progress, being washed of all contaminations, then ultimately, achieving perfection after many, many births of practice, that person attains the supreme goal.

"A yogi is greater than the ascetic, greater than the empiricist, and greater than the fruitive worker. Therefore, O Arjuna, in all circumstances, be a yogi. And of all yogis, those with great faith who always abide in Me, think of Me within their hearts, and render transcendental loving service to Me—they are the most intimately united with Me in yoga and are the highest of all. That is My opinion."

Everyone is part and parcel of the Supreme Person, and thus everyone is intended to serve the Supreme Lord constitutionally. Failing to do this, one neglects one's duty and falls down. Here, at the end of the Sixth Chapter, Krishna informs us that the culmination of all kinds of yoga practice lies in *bhakti-yoga*, or transcendental loving service to Him. All other yogas are but means to come to the point of *bhakti* in *bhakti-yoga*. *Karma-yoga*, to work without fruitive results, is the beginning of this path. When *karma-yoga* increases in knowledge and renunciation, the stage is called *jnana-yoga*. When *jnana-yoga* increases in meditation on the Supersoul by different physical processes, and the mind is fixed on Him, it is called *astanga-yoga*. And when one surpasses *astanga-yoga* and comes to the point of the Supreme Person, Krishna, it is called *bhakti-yoga*, the highest stage of yoga and the ultimate goal.

7

Knowledge of the Absolute

IN THE FIRST SIX CHAPTERS of the *Bhagavad-gita*, Krishna has described the living entity as a nonmaterial spirit soul capable of elevating itself to self-realization by different types of yoga. At the end of Chapter Six, Krishna clearly states that the steady concentration of the mind upon Him, or in other words, Krishna consciousness, is the highest form of all yoga. In the next six chapters, Krishna will reveal scientific knowledge of Himself and the eternal relationship of the living entities with Him—revelations understood by the practice of *bhakti-yoga*.

The Supreme Lord
"Now hear, O Arjuna, how by practicing yoga in full consciousness of Me, with mind attached to Me, you can know Me in full, free from doubt." In the previous chapter, Arjuna declined to concentrate his mind through *astanga-yoga*; now Krishna tells him that he can advance in God consciousness through attachment to God.

"I shall now declare unto you in full this knowledge, both material and spiritual. This being known, nothing further shall remain for you to know.

"Out of many thousands of people, one may endeavor for perfection, and of those who have achieved perfection, hardly one knows Me in truth." Only pure devotees can know something of the inconceivable transcendental qualities of Krishna, of His omnipotence and opulence, and of His wealth, fame, strength, beauty, knowledge, and renunciation,

By watering the root of a tree, we water the whole tree—
the twigs, branches, leaves, fruits, and flowers. Similarly, by
loving Krishna we distribute our love to all living beings.

because Krishna reveals Himself to the devotees, being pleased with them for their transcendental loving service to Him.

As promised, Krishna describes His various energies. "Earth, water, fire, air, ether, mind, intelligence, and false ego—all together these eight constitute My separated material energies. Besides these, O mighty-armed Arjuna, there is another, superior energy of Mine, which comprises the living entities who are exploiting the resources of this material, inferior nature." This material world is a temporary manifestation of one of the energies of the Lord. Generally those who do not know the science of God assume that this material world is meant for their own pleasure and that human beings are the causes, controllers, and enjoyers of the material energy.

According to *Bhagavad-gita*, this atheistic conclusion is false. The Supreme Lord Krishna is the only controller, and He controls both the inferior (material) energy and the superior (spiritual) energy. As living entities we are His superior energy because the quality of our existence is one with the Supreme, but we are never equal to the Lord in quantity of power.

While exploiting the gross and subtle inferior energies, one forgets one's spiritual mind and intelligence and identifies oneself as the material body. This forgetfulness is due to the influence of matter upon us. But when we become free from the influence of the illusory material energy, we are liberated from all material ideas, including the conception of becoming one in all respects with God.

"All created beings have their source in these two natures. Of all that is material and all that is spiritual in this world, know for certain that I am both the origin and dissolution." Everything that exists is a product of matter and spirit. This material body develops because spirit is present within matter; a child grows gradually to become a

The Lord says that water, earth,
air—the basic ingredients of
this planet—are His energy.

The taste of pure water is one of God's energies.

teenager and then an adult because that superior energy, the soul, is present. Similarly, the entire universe develops because of the presence of Krishna as the Supersoul.

"O conqueror of wealth, there is no truth superior to Me. Everything rests upon Me, as pearls are strung on a thread. O Arjuna, I am the taste of water, the light of the sun and the moon, the syllable *om* in the Vedic mantras; I am the sound in ether and ability in people." Although the Lord is in His eternal abode, we can perceive Him by His all-pervading diverse energies.

"I am the original fragrance of the earth, and I am the heat in fire. I am the life of all that lives, and I am the penances of all ascetics. I am the original seed of all existences, the intelligence of the intelligent, and the prowess of all powerful people.

"I am the strength of the strong, devoid of passion and desire. I am sex life which is not contrary to religious principles, O Arjuna."

The strong person should apply his strength to protect the weak, not for personal aggression. Sex life, according to religious principles, should be only for the propagation of children, and the parents' responsibility is then to help their children become godly.

"Know that all states of being—be they goodness, passion or ignorance—are manifested by My energy. I am, in one sense, everything, but I am independent. I am not under the modes of material nature, for they, on the contrary, are within Me." All material activities in the world are being conducted under the three modes of material nature—goodness, passion, and ignorance—which are emanations from the Supreme Lord. However, He is neither subjected to nor affected by these modes.

"Deluded by goodness, passion, and ignorance, the whole world does not know Me, I who am above the modes and inexhaustible." The whole world is enchanted by these three modes of material nature and thus cannot understand that transcendental to this material nature is the Supreme Lord, Krishna.

Every living entity under the influence of material nature has a particular type of body, each with its own psychological and biological activities accordingly. Although material nature is an inferior energy, it emanates from and is conducted by Krishna's divine will, and it acts so wonderfully that to get release from its clutches is difficult.

"This divine energy of Mine, consisting of the three modes of material nature, is difficult to overcome. But those who have surrendered unto Me can easily cross beyond it."

Krishna then describes four kinds of misdirected people who refuse to surrender to the Supreme: (1) those who are grossly foolish, (2) those who are socially and politically developed, but have no religious principles, (3) great philosophers, poets, literati, scientists, and others who deride God, considering Him merely another human being, and (4) those who are openly atheistic. Some atheists argue that the Supreme Lord can never descend into this material world, but they are unable to give any tangible reasons as to why not. Others make Him subordinate to His impersonal feature, although Krishna declares the opposite in the *Gita*. Envious of the Supreme Person, they cannot surrender to Him. Thus, these four types of impious people never surrender to the Supreme Lord, in spite of all scriptural and authoritative advice.

"O Arjuna, four types of pious people begin to render devotional service unto Me—the distressed, the desirers of wealth, the sometimes inquisitive, and those who are searching for knowledge of the Absolute."

The humble ass works hard and is satisfied merely by filling his stomach. Thus he is like the foolish worker who does not know for whom he should work or why. Sometimes this worker may bray of poetry and philosophy, but such sounds only disturb others.

As a policeman is empowered by the government he serves, demigods are empowered by the Supreme Lord.

Those who are always busy with fruitive activities come to the Lord in material distress and then associate with pure devotees and become, in their distress, devotees of the Lord. Those who are simply frustrated also come sometimes to associate with pure devotees and become inquisitive to know about God. Similarly, when dry philosophers are frustrated in every field of knowledge, they sometimes want to learn of God, and they come to the Supreme Lord to render devotional service. "Of these, those who are in full knowledge and who are always engaged in pure devotional service are the best. For I am very dear to them, and they are dear to Me.

"All these devotees are undoubtedly magnanimous souls, but those who are situated in knowledge of Me I consider to be just like My own self. Being engaged in My transcendental service, they are sure to attain Me, the highest and most perfect goal.

"After many births and deaths, one who is actually in knowledge surrenders unto Me, knowing Me to be the cause of all causes and all that is. Such a great soul is very rare.

"Those whose intelligence has been stolen by material desires surrender unto demigods and follow the particular rules and regulations of worship according to their own natures. I am in everyone's heart as the Supersoul. As soon as one desires to worship some demigod, I make his faith steady so that he can devote himself to that particular deity. Endowed with such a faith, he endeavors to worship a particular demigod and obtains his desires. But in actuality these benefits are bestowed by Me alone." The demigods are powerful universal administrators who can bestow material benedictions upon those who worship them. Thus less intelligent people who have lost their spiritual sense take shelter of demigods for immediate fulfillment of material desires. Devotees, however, depend on the Supreme Lord for the satisfaction of their material needs, and are satisfied with whatever the Lord gives.

One may ask why all-powerful God gives facilities to the living entities for enjoying this world and lets them fall into the trap of the material energy. The answer is that if the Supreme Lord as Supersoul does not give such facilities, then there is no meaning to independence. Therefore He gives everyone full independence—whatever one likes—but His ultimate instruction in the *Bhagavad-gita* is: one should give up all other engagements and fully surrender unto Him. That will lead to happiness.

"People of small intelligence worship the demigods, and their fruits are limited and temporary. Those who worship the demigods go to the planets of the demigods, but My devotees ultimately reach My supreme planet.

"Unintelligent people, who do not know Me perfectly, think that I, the Supreme Lord, Krishna, was impersonal before and have now assumed this personality. Due to their small knowledge, they do not know My higher nature, which is imperishable and supreme." As demigod worshipers are less intelligent, so, too, are impersonalists—those who think that the Supreme Absolute Truth ultimately has no form. The impersonal feature is one of the Lord's aspects, as sunshine is an energy of the sun. Supreme realization may begin from this impersonal feature and then rise to the localized Supersoul—but the ultimate word in the Absolute Truth is the Supreme Person, Lord Krishna. Without devotional service and without the development of Krishna consciousness, this fact remains hidden from the impersonalists as they speculate to understand the Absolute.

"I am never manifest to the foolish and unintelligent. For them I am covered by My internal potency, and therefore they do not know that I am unborn and infallible.

"O Arjuna, as the Supreme Lord, I know everything that has happened in the past, all that is happening in the present, and all things that are yet to come. I also know all living entities; but Me no one knows.

"O conqueror of the foe, all living entities are born into delusion, bewildered by dualities arisen from desire and hate." The constitutional position of the living entity is that of subordination to the Supreme Lord, but when one is deluded, one becomes controlled by God's material energy. Then, instead of understanding the Lord, the ignorant person envies Him and strives to become one with Him.

"Those who have acted piously in previous lives and in this life and whose sinful actions are completely eradicated are freed from dualities and engage in My service with determination." For those who are sinful, atheistic, foolish, and deceitful, it is very difficult to transcend the dualities of material nature and advance spiritually.

But, Krishna says, "Those in full consciousness of Me, who know Me, the Supreme Lord, to be the governing principle of the material manifestation, of the demigods, and of all methods of sacrifice, can understand and know Me, the Supreme Person, even at the time of death."

Chapter Seven in particular explains how one can become fully Krishna conscious, first by associating with those who are Krishna conscious, and then by understanding that Krishna is the Supreme Person. At the same time one can understand the constitutional position of the living entity and how the living entity forgets Krishna and becomes entangled in material activities. Krishna conscious persons directly engage in activities of Krishna consciousness and thereby factually attain their constitutional positions as eternal servitors of God. In that state they take pleasure in hearing about and glorifying the Supreme Lord and are convinced that by so doing, they will fulfill all their objectives.

When the sky is reflected in water, the reflections represent both the stars and the moon. The stars may be compared to the living entities, and the moon to the Supreme Lord. The Lord is the greatest Being, and the living entities are eternally small, both in the spiritual world and in its reflection, the material world.

8

Attaining the Supreme

Arjuna

O MY LORD, O SUPREME PERSON, what is Brahman? What is the self? What are fruitive activities? What is this material manifestation? And what are the demigods? Please explain this to me.
"Who is the Lord of sacrifice, and how does He live in the body, O Krishna? And how can those engaged in devotional service know You at the time of death?"

The Supreme Lord
"The indestructible, transcendental living entity is called Brahman [the individual soul], and its eternal nature is called the self. Action pertaining to the development of the material bodies of the living entities is called karma, or fruitive activities." Krishna is answering Arjuna's questions one by one. He explains that, under the influence of material consciousness, the living entity (Brahman) has to take on various bodies in the material world. That is karma, or varied creation by the force of material consciousness.

"The physical nature, which is constantly changing, is called the material manifestation. The universal form of the Lord includes all the demigods, like those of the sun and moon, and I, the Supreme Lord, represented as the Supersoul in the heart of every embodied being, am called the Lord of sacrifice." The Supersoul, who is nondifferent from the Supreme Lord Himself, is situated in the heart of every living entity beside the individual soul, as the witness of the individual soul's activities.

At the time of death, the soul—represented by the bird—leaves the cage of the body. As explained in this chapter, where the soul journeys depends on its consciousness.

*Our thoughts at death result from our thoughts during life. Our final
thoughts carry us—each soul—to the body we shall have next.*

After briefly answering six of Arjuna's questions, the Lord answers at
length his seventh and final question.

"Whoever, at the end of life, quits the body remembering Me alone, at
once attains My nature. Of this there is no doubt." Those who die with
their consciousness fixed on Krishna are at once transferred to the transcendental nature of the Supreme Lord. This remembrance of Krishna is
possible for those who have been Krishna conscious during their life-
times. Therefore, if we want to achieve success at the end of our lives,
the process of remembering God is essential, and to this end devotees
chant the Lord's holy names, which reawakens their God consciousness.
The thoughts during our lives accumulate to influence our thoughts at
the moment of death. In this way our present life creates our next life, as
Lord Krishna explains: "Whatever state of being one remembers when
one quits the body, O Arjuna, that state one will attain without fail.
Therefore, Arjuna, you should always think of Me and at the same time
carry out your prescribed duty of fighting. With your activities dedicated
to Me and your mind and intelligence fixed on Me, you will attain Me
without doubt." If one is transcendentally absorbed in God's service,

then one's next body will be transcendental, not material. The Lord does not say we should abandon our prescribed duties or engagements. We can continue them and at the same time think of God. This will free us from material contamination and engage our minds and intelligence in God.

"One who meditates on Me as the Supreme Person, with the mind constantly engaged in remembering Me, undeviating from the path, that person, O Arjuna, is sure to reach Me.

"One should meditate upon the Supreme Person as the one who knows everything, as He who is the oldest, who is the controller, who is smaller than the smallest, who is the maintainer of everything, who is beyond all material conception, who is inconceivable, and who is always a person. He is luminous like the sun, and He is transcendental, beyond this material nature." The Supreme Lord is a person, but not an ordinary person. He is beyond the imagination, beyond the mind's jurisdiction, and beyond the reach of all argument, logic, and philosophical speculation. Therefore He is inconceivable, and His devotees, avoiding useless argument, accept the statements of the scriptures and follow the principles therein.

"One who, at the time of death, fixes the life air between the eyebrows and, by the strength of yoga, with an undeviating mind, engages in remembering the

As a mannequin imitates a higher reality—a person— so this material world imitates the spiritual one.

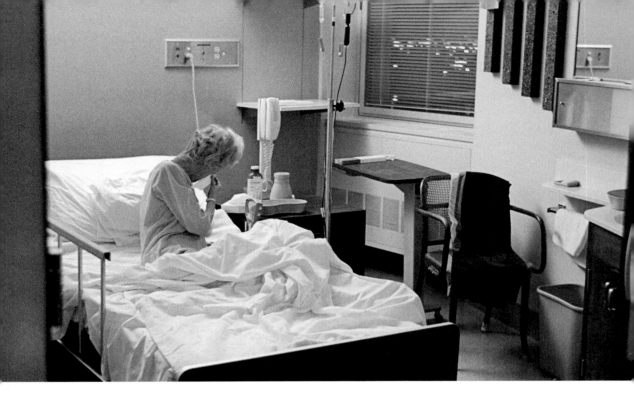

Supreme Lord in full devotion, will certainly attain to the Supreme Lord."

"For those who always remember Me without deviation, I am easy to obtain, O Arjuna, because of their constant engagement in devotional service." Perfect devotees have no desire other than to please the Supreme Lord. Such devotees are always constantly engaged in the transcendental loving service of the Supreme Lord, and so for them the Lord is easily attained; they cannot forget the Supreme Lord for a moment, and similarly the Supreme Lord cannot forget His pure devotees for a moment.

"After attaining Me, the great souls, who are yogis in devotion, never return to this temporary world, which is full of miseries, because they have attained the highest perfection. From the highest planet in the material world down to the lowest, all are places of misery wherein repeated birth and death take place. But one who attains My abode, O Arjuna, never takes birth again." Since this temporary material world is full of the miseries of birth, old age, disease, and death, naturally the person who attains God's kingdom does not wish to return. As God is

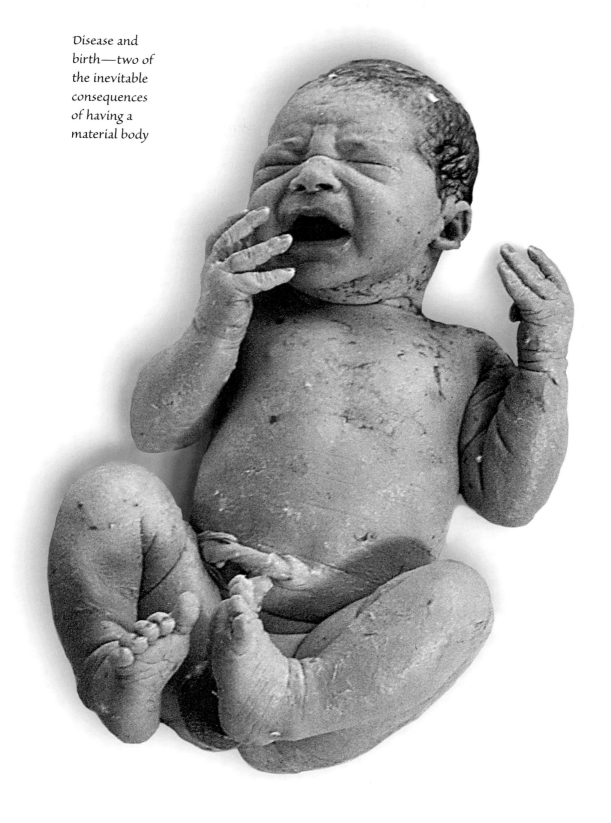

Disease and birth—two of the inevitable consequences of having a material body transcendental and eternal, so is His kingdom. It is beyond all the periodic manifestations and annihilations of material nature.

All kinds of yogis eventually have to attain devotional perfection in *bhakti-yoga* or God consciousness before they can go to His transcendental abode and remain eternally. Those who attain the highest material planets, the planets of the demigods, are again subjected to repeated birth and death.

"The Supreme Person, who is greater than all, is attainable by unalloyed devotion. Although He is present in His abode, He is all-pervading, and everything is within Him." In the Lord's supreme abode, nothing is material. All the variegatedness therein is the spiritual expansion of the Supreme Lord Himself. As far as this material world is concerned, although the Lord is always in His supreme abode, He is nonetheless all-pervading by His material energy. So by His spiritual and material energies He is present everywhere—in both the material and the spiritual universes.

"A person who accepts the path of devotional service is not bereft of the results derived from studying the *Vedas*, performing austere sacrifices, giving in charity, or pursuing philosophical and fruitive activities. Simply by performing devotional service, that person attains all these, and at the end reaches the supreme eternal abode." The beauty of Krishna consciousness is that by one stroke, by engaging in devotional service, we can surpass all the rituals of the different orders of life. We should try to understand this not by scholarship or mental speculation but by hearing about Krishna in association with devotees.

We can learn the *Bhagavad-gita* from a devotee, for no one else perfectly understands the purpose of the *Bhagavad-gita*. By such advancement in the association of the devotee, one is placed in devotional service and this service at once will dispel all one's misgivings about God and His activities, forms, pastimes, names, and other features. Then one becomes fixed in one's study, relishes that study, and always feels God conscious. In the advanced stage, one falls completely in love with God. This highest perfectional stage of life enables devotees to be transferred to the Lord's abode in the spiritual sky, where they become eternally happy.

As one can smell the fragrance of a rose by being near it, so the Supersoul—the Lord, seated in the heart next to the soul—knows the soul's innermost desires.

9

The Most Confidential Knowledge

KNOWLEDGE CONCERNING the eternal, constitutional activity of the soul, which is *bhakti*, or transcendental devotional service to God, is the most confidential knowledge because, although this knowledge is available to all, only a devotee will accept it. This is the subject of this chapter.

The Supreme Lord
"My dear Arjuna, because you are never envious of Me, I shall impart to you this most confidential knowledge and realization; knowing this you shall be relieved of the miseries of material existence." Simply to understand that a living entity is ultimately spiritual is insufficient. That is the beginning of spiritual realization, but we should recognize the difference between the activities of those who are bodily conscious and the activities of those who are spiritually conscious.

"This knowledge is the king of education, the most secret of all secrets. It is the purest knowledge, and because it gives direct perception of the self by realization, it is the perfection of religion." There are huge universities all over the world with many departments of knowledge. But there is, unfortunately, no university or educational institution that

A woman with a paramour does her duties carefully, so that her husband won't suspect her attachment. Similarly, devotees always remember the supreme lover, Krishna, while seeing to their material duties.

teaches the science of the spirit soul. Yet the soul is the most important part of the body; without the presence of the soul, the body has no value. Still people are placing all their energies on the bodily necessities of life, not caring for the vital soul.

The knowledge of which Krishna speaks leads to devotional service, a happy and sublime process, which, in His words, is "everlasting and joyfully performed." One can simply hear the chanting of the glories of the Lord or attend philosophical lectures on transcendental knowledge given by bona fide spiritual teachers. Simply by sitting, one can learn; then one can eat palatable food that has been offered to God. The prerequisite for this service isn't wealth, erudition, or an aristocratic birth, but only faith.

"Those who are not faithful in this devotional service cannot attain Me, O conqueror of enemies. Therefore they return to the path of birth and death in this material world." Faith is the conviction that simply by serving the Supreme Lord one can achieve all perfection.

"By Me, in My unmanifested form [the impersonal energy of Lord Krishna], this entire universe is pervaded. All beings are in Me, but I [the Supreme Person, Lord Krishna] am not in them." Just as the sunshine spreads throughout the universe, the Lord's energy is present throughout the creation, and everything is resting in that energy. Yet we should not conclude that because He pervades the universe He has lost His personal existence. For example, a king heads a government that is representative of the king's energy; the different governmental departments manifest the energies of the king, and each department is resting on the king's power. However, one cannot expect the king to be personally present in every department. Similarly, all the manifestations that we see and everything that exists, both in this material world and in the spiritual world, are resting on the effulgence of the Supreme Person.

"And yet everything that is created does not rest in Me. Behold My mystic opulence! Although I am the maintainer of all living entities and although I am everywhere, I am not a part of this cosmic manifestation, for My Self is the very source of creation.

"Understand that as the mighty wind, blowing everywhere, rests always in the sky, all created beings rest in Me. O Arjuna, at the end of the millennium all material manifestations enter into My nature, and at the beginning of another millennium, by My potency, I create them again.

"The whole cosmic order is under Me. Under My will it is automatically manifested again and again, and under My will it is annihilated at the end.

"O Arjuna, all this work cannot bind Me. I am ever detached from all these material activities, seated as though neutral." In His spiritual world the Supreme Lord engages in His eternal, blissful, spiritual activities; He has nothing to do with material activities. Those are being carried on by His different potencies.

"This material nature, which is one of My energies, is working under My direction, O Arjuna, producing all moving and nonmoving beings. Under its rule this manifestation is created and annihilated again and again." Material nature, without the superintendence of the Supreme Lord, can do nothing. Yet the Supreme Lord is detached from all material activity.

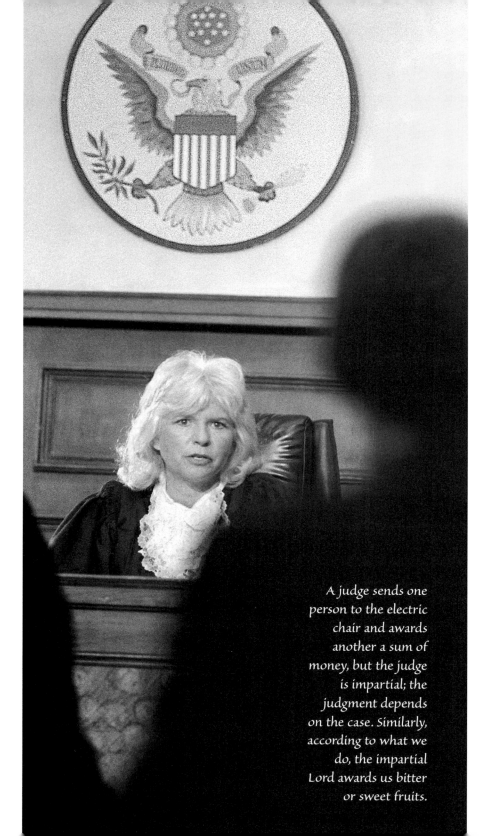

A judge sends one person to the electric chair and awards another a sum of money, but the judge is impartial; the judgment depends on the case. Similarly, according to what we do, the impartial Lord awards us bitter or sweet fruits.

"Fools deride Me when I descend in the human form. They do not know My transcendental nature as the Supreme Lord of all. Those who are thus bewildered are attracted by demonic and atheistic views. In that deluded condition, their hopes for liberation, their fruitive activities, and their culture of knowledge are all defeated."

Despite the transcendental qualities of Lord Krishna's body, its full bliss, knowledge, and eternality, many so-called scholars and commentators of *Bhagavad-gita* deride Krishna as an ordinary man. They do not understand that He controls the powerful material energy and that whoever surrenders unto Him can escape the influence of this material energy. If by surrendering to Krishna a soul can avoid the effects of material energy, then how can the Supreme Lord, who conducts the creation, maintenance, and annihilation of the whole cosmic manifestation have a material body like us? This idea is foolish.

"O Arjuna, those who are not deluded, the great souls, are under the protection of the divine nature. They are fully engaged in devotional service because they know Me as the Supreme Person, original and inexhaustible. Always chanting My glories, endeavoring with great determination, bowing down before Me, these great souls perpetually worship Me with devotion.

"Others, who engage in sacrifice by the cultivation of knowledge, worship the Supreme Lord as the one without a second, as diverse in many, and in the universal form." The Lord explains to Arjuna that those who are purely God conscious, who see His presence in all things and events, are called great souls (*mahatmas*); yet others who are not *mahatmas* also worship God. Krishna has described some of them as the distressed, the financially destitute, the inquisitive, and the seekers of knowledge. Still others, who are lower, are divided into three groups: (1) monists or impersonalists who worship themselves as one with the Supreme Lord, (2) idolators who concoct some form of the Lord and worship that, and (3) those who accept the material universe and, therefore, the universal form of the Lord as supreme, and worship that.

"I am the goal, the sustainer, the master, the witness, the abode, the refuge, and the most dear friend. I am the creation and the annihilation, the basis of everything, the resting place, and the eternal seed. O

Arjuna, I give heat, and I withhold and send forth the rain. I am immortality, and I am also death personified. Both spirit and matter are in Me." By analyzing all of God's different energies, one can understand that for Him there is no distinction between matter and spirit. In the advanced stage of God consciousness, one therefore makes no such distinctions. A pure devotee sees only God in everything.

"Those who always worship Me with exclusive devotion, meditating on My transcendental form—to them I carry what they lack, and I preserve what they have." The Lord helps the devotees achieve God consciousness, and when they become fully God conscious, the Lord protects them from a miserable conditioned life.

"Those who are devotees of other gods and who worship them with faith actually worship only Me, O Arjuna, but they do so in a wrong way. I am the only enjoyer and master of all sacrifices. Therefore, those who do not recognize My true transcendental nature fall down. Those who worship the demigods will take birth among the demigods; those who worship the ancestors will go to the ancestors; those who worship ghosts and spirits will take birth among such beings; and those who worship Me will live with Me.

"If one offers Me with love and devotion a leaf, a flower, a fruit, or water, I will accept it." The process of Krishna consciousness is so easy that we can offer even a leaf or a little water or fruit to the Supreme Lord in genuine love, and the Lord will be pleased to accept it. No one, therefore, can be barred from Krishna consciousness, because it is so simple and universal. Krishna wants only loving service and nothing more. He needs nothing from anyone, because He is self-sufficient, and yet He accepts the offering of His devotee in an exchange of love and affection. This love and devotion (bhakti) is the only means by which to approach Him.

One who loves Krishna will give Him whatever pleases Him, and so a devotee avoids offering undesirable or unwanted things. Thus the devotee does not offer meat, fish, and eggs to Krishna. If He desired such things as offerings, He would have said so here. Vegetables, grains, fruits, milk, and water are the proper foods for human beings, and Lord Krishna Himself prescribes them.

When a child lovingly offers
her father a cracker, her father,
who has no need for the
cracker, is happy to accept it. In
the same way, God is pleased
when we first offer Him the
food He has kindly provided.

As soon as a child comes
to the arms of her mother,
the child's tears stop; she is
happy. Similarly, when we
love God we will feel
completely happy .

Impersonalist philosophers, who believe that the Absolute Truth is without senses, cannot understand how the Lord eats. In actuality, Krishna, the Supreme Lord, has senses, and His senses are interchangeable; in other words, one sense can perform the function of any other. This is what it means to say that Krishna is absolute. Lacking senses, He could hardly be considered full in all opulences. Krishna's hearing His devotee's words of love in the offering of food is wholly identical with His eating and tasting.

"Whatever you do, whatever you eat, whatever you offer or give away, and whatever austerities you perform—do that, O Arjuna, as an offering to Me. In this way you will be freed from bondage to work and its auspicious and inauspicious results. With your mind fixed on Me in this principle of renunciation, you will be liberated and come to Me.

"I envy no one, nor am I partial to anyone. I am equal to all. But those who render service unto Me in devotion are friends, are in Me, and I am also a friend to them.

"Even those who commit the most abominable action, if they are engaged in devotional service they are considered saintly because they are properly situated in their determination." Material contamination is so strong that even a yogi fully absorbed in the service of the Lord sometimes becomes ensnared; but Krishna consciousness is so strong that such an occasional lapse into bodily identification is at once rectified. No one should deride a devotee for some accidental lapse. On the other hand, we should not think that a devotee can act in all kinds of abominable ways; this statement by Krishna only refers to an accident due to the strong power of material connections.

"They quickly become righteous and attain lasting peace. O Arjuna, declare it boldly that My devotees never perish.

"O Arjuna, those who take shelter in Me, though they be of lower birth, can attain the supreme destination. Therefore, having come to this temporary world, engage in loving service unto Me." Here the Supreme Lord clearly makes no distinction between lower and higher classes of people engaged in His devotional service. Such divisions exist in the material conception of life, but not for a person engaged in the Lord's transcendental service. Through this pure loving service, everyone can become attached to God, and anyone may enter His kingdom. Devotional service to the Supreme Lord is the process by which all people can solve all problems.

"Engage your mind always in thinking of Me, become My devotee, offer obeisances to Me, and worship Me. Being completely absorbed in Me, surely you will come to Me." Unscrupulous commentators distort the meaning of what is clearly stated here. They divert the reader by distinguishing between Krishna's mind and Krishna, but His body, His mind, and He Himself are one and absolute.

Krishna is the Absolute Truth. His body is not material but is eternal, blissful knowledge, and one should therefore engage the mind in the eternal form of Krishna. With conviction in one's heart that Krishna is the Supreme, one should engage oneself in worship and thus become fully absorbed in Him without deviation. Such a person will eventually achieve the supreme award of Krishna.

When a mother sees her child's shoes, she remembers the child she loves. In the same way, when the Lord's pure devotees see anything in this world, they are reminded of their beloved Lord.

94

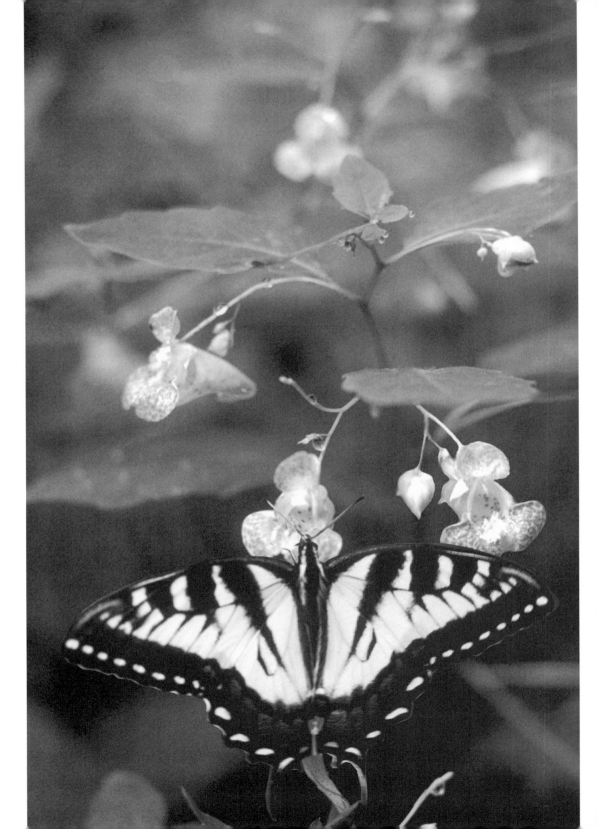

10

The Opulence of the Absolute

The Supreme Lord

LISTEN AGAIN, O MIGHTY-ARMED ARJUNA. Because you are My dear friend, for your benefit I shall speak to you further." In this chapter, Krishna will explain His specific opulences, manifested through His all-pervasive energies.

"Neither the demigods nor the sages know My origin or opulences, for, in every respect, I am the source of the demigods and sages. One who knows Me as the unborn, as the beginningless, as the Supreme Lord of all the worlds—that person only is freed from all sins.

"One who is factually convinced of My opulence and mystic power engages in unalloyed devotional service; of this there is no doubt." If we know factually how great God is, then naturally we become surrendered souls and engage in the devotional service of the Lord. We should not neglect understanding Krishna's greatness, for by knowing this we will become fixed in sincere devotional service.

"I am the source of all spiritual and material worlds. Everything emanates from Me. The wise who perfectly know this engage in My devotional service and worship Me with all their hearts.

"The thoughts of My pure devotees dwell in Me, their lives are fully devoted to My service, and they derive great satisfaction and bliss from always enlightening one another and conversing about Me. To those who are constantly devoted to serving Me with love, I give the understanding by which they can come to Me. To show them special mercy,

God's opulences are the smallest wonders and the greatest majesties of our world.

I, dwelling in their hearts, destroy with the shining lamp of knowledge the darkness born of ignorance."

Sometimes philosophers criticize devotees as being naive sentimentalists. Actually, this is not the fact. There are very, very learned scholars who have expounded the philosophy of devotion. But even if some devotees are not learned scholars, if they are sincere in their devotional service, they are enlightened by God Himself within their hearts. The Supreme Truth is so great that it is not possible to understand Him or to achieve Him simply by mental effort. Only by devotional service is the Supreme Truth, Krishna, pleased, and only then by His inconceivable energy will He reveal Himself to the pure devotee.

Arjuna

"You are the Supreme Person, the ultimate abode, the purest, the Absolute Truth. You are the eternal, transcendental, original person, the unborn, the greatest. All the great sages such as Narada, Asita, Devala, and Vyasa confirm this truth about You, and now You Yourself are declaring it to me.

"O Krishna, I totally accept as truth all that You have told me. Neither the demigods nor the demons, O Lord, can understand Your personality. Indeed, You alone know Yourself by Your own internal potency, O Supreme Person, origin of all, Lord of all beings, God of gods, Lord of the universe!" We should emulate Arjuna's acceptance of Krishna's statements; then we can understand the essence of the *Bhagavad-gita*, and only then can we understand that Krishna is the Supreme Person.

"Please tell me in detail of Your divine opulences by which You pervade all these worlds. O Krishna, O supreme mystic, how shall I constantly think of You, and how shall I know You? In what various forms shall I remember You, O Supreme Person? Again please describe in detail the mystic power of Your opulences. I am never satiated in hearing about You, for the more I hear the more I want to taste the nectar of Your words." Arjuna has no doubt about Krishna's supremacy, but he wants to know how the common person can understand the all-pervading Lord. Common people who have no love for God cannot always think of Him; therefore they have to think materially. Because materialists cannot understand Krishna spiritually, Krishna advises them to concentrate their minds on physical things and try to see how He manifests through physical representations.

The Supreme Lord
"Yes, I will tell you of My splendorous manifestations, but only of those which are prominent, O Arjuna, for My opulence is limitless." It is impossible to comprehend Krishna's greatness or His opulences with our material senses. Thus the Lord begins describing what we can directly perceive—representations that give a hint of His greatness.

"Of lights I am the radiant sun. Of the senses I am the mind, and in living beings I am consciousness. Of bodies of water I am the ocean; of vibrations I am the

Of lights He is the sun, and of bodies of water He is the ocean.

transcendental *om*." Of all the transcendental vibrations, the sacred syllable *om (omkara)* represents Krishna. "Of sacrifices I am the chanting of the holy names *[japa]*." Of all sacrifices, the chanting of Krishna's holy names is the purest representation of God. "Of immovable things I am the Himalayas." Whatever is sublime in the world is a representation of Krishna. Therefore the Himalayas, the greatest mountains in the world, also represent Him.

"Of all trees I am the banyan tree, and of the sages among the demigods I am Narada. Among subduers I am inexhaustible time, among beasts I am the lion, and among birds I am Garuda." The banyan tree is one of the highest and most beautiful trees. Narada is considered the greatest devotee in the universe, thus Krishna chooses him as the representation of a pure devotee. Among many subduing principles, time wears down all things in the material universe and so represents Krishna. Of animals, the lion is the most powerful and ferocious, and of the million varieties of birds, Garuda, the bearer of Lord Vishnu, is the greatest.

If death is like a cat, then a devotee is like a kitten, carried to safety.

Of seasons, Krishna is flower-bearing spring.

"Of purifiers I am the wind, of the wielders of weapons I am Rama, of fishes I am the shark, and of flowing rivers I am the Ganges." Of all the aquatics the shark is one of the biggest and is certainly the most dangerous to man. Thus the shark represents Krishna.

"Of all creations I am the beginning and the end and also the middle, O Arjuna. Of all sciences I am the spiritual science of the self, and among logicians I am the conclusive truth. I am all-devouring death, and I am the generating principle of all that is yet to be. Among women I am fame, fortune, fine speech, memory, intelligence, steadfastness, and patience." When a person is fully qualified, yet humble and gentle, and when she is able to keep her balance both in sorrow and in the ecstasy of joy, she has the opulence called patience.

"Of seasons I am flower-bearing spring. I am also the gambling of cheats." There are many kinds of cheaters, but of all cheating processes, gambling stands supreme and therefore represents Krishna. As the Supreme, Krishna can be more deceitful than any mere mortal. If Krishna chooses to deceive a person, no one can surpass Him in His deceit. His greatness is not simply one-sided—it is all-sided.

"Of the splendid I am the splendor. I am victory, I am adventure, and I am the strength of the strong." He is

101

the most splendorous of all. Among the enterprising and industrious, He is the most enterprising, the most industrious. No one can surpass Him.

"Among all means of suppressing lawlessness I am punishment, and of those who seek victory I am morality." When miscreants are punished, the agency of chastisement represents Krishna. In any attempt at being victorious in some field of activity, the greatest element is morality.

"Of secret things I am silence, and of the wise I am the wisdom." Among the confidential activities of hearing, thinking, and meditating,

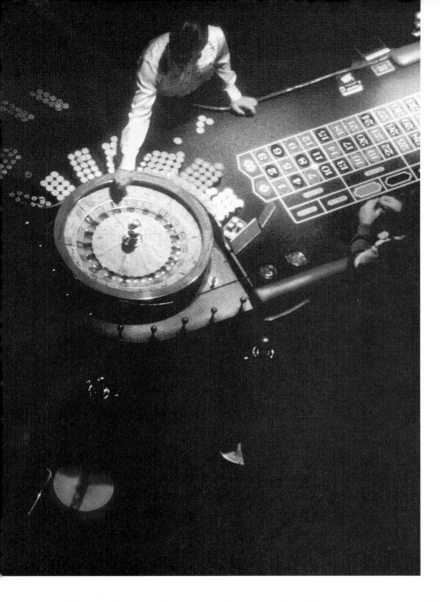

God's greatness is not simply onesided—it is all-sided. If He chooses to deceive a person, no one can surpass Him in His deceit. And of all forms of cheating, gambling stands supreme and therefore represents Krishna.

silence is most important because by silence one can make progress quickly. The wise person is one who can discriminate between matter and spirit, between God's inferior and superior natures. Such knowledge is Krishna Himself. "Furthermore, O Arjuna, I am the generating seed of all existences. There is no being—moving or nonmoving—that can exist without Me. O mighty conqueror of enemies, there is no end to My divine manifestations. What I have spoken to you is but a mere indication of My infinite opulences.

"Know that all opulent, beautiful, and glorious creations spring from but a spark of My splendor. But what need is there, Arjuna, for all this detailed knowledge? With a single fragment of Myself I pervade and support this entire universe." The Supersoul enters into all things and represents the Supreme Lord throughout the material universes. The Lord here tells Arjuna that there is no point in understanding how anything exists in its separate opulence and grandeur; all things are existing, from the most gigantic entity down to the smallest ant, due to His entering them as Supersoul, and all are sustained by Him. Therefore Lord

11

The Universal Form

Arjuna

BY MY HEARING THE INSTRUCTIONS You have kindly given me about these most confidential spiritual subjects, my illusion has now been dispelled. O lotus-eyed one, I have heard from You in detail about the appearance and disappearance of every living entity and have realized Your inexhaustible glories." Now Arjuna no longer sees Krishna as merely a human being, or only as his friend, but rather as the source of everything. Arjuna is enlightened. He is glad to have such a great friend as Krishna, but he thinks that, while he accepts Krishna as the source of everything, others may not. So to establish Krishna's divinity for all, in this chapter he requests that Krishna show His universal form.

"O greatest of all personalities, O supreme form, though I see You here before me in Your actual position, as You have described Yourself, I wish to see how You have entered into this cosmic manifestation. I want to see that form of Yours. If You think that I am able to behold Your cosmic form, O my Lord, O master of all mystic power, then kindly show me that unlimited universal Self." Arjuna, as a devotee, does not depend on his speculative strength; rather, he admits his limitations as a living entity and acknowledges Krishna's inestimable position. Arjuna knows that the infinitesimal living entity cannot understand the unlimited infinite. If the infinite reveals Himself, only then is it possible to understand the nature of the infinite, by the grace of the infinite.

If you have a loving father who is a policeman, one day you may see him in action, firing his revolver. At that time, awe and fear overcome your love. In the same way, when Arjuna saw Krishna's cosmic form, he was frightened. Thus he requested Krishna to appear again in a form he could love.

The Supreme Person
"My dear Arjuna, see now My opulences, hundreds of thousands of varied divine and multicolored forms. See here the different manifestations of all the demigods. Behold the many wonderful things which no one has ever seen or heard of before.

108

If hundreds of thousands of suns were to rise at once into the sky, their radiance might resemble the effulgence of the Supreme Person in His universal form.

"O Arjuna, whatever you wish to see, behold at once in this body of Mine! This universal form can show you whatever you now desire to see and whatever you may want to see in the future. Everything—moving and nonmoving—is here completely, in one place.

"But you cannot see Me with your present eyes. Therefore I give you divine eyes. Behold My mystic opulence!" For his own conviction, Arjuna doesn't need to see Krishna's universal form, however he asks to see it so that in the future, people would understand that Krishna presented Himself as the Supreme to Arjuna, not only theoretically and philosophically, but also in actuality.

Sanjaya
"O Dhritarastra, having spoken thus, the Supreme Lord of all mystic power, the Supreme Person, displayed His universal form to Arjuna. Arjuna saw in that universal form unlimited mouths, unlimited eyes, unlimited wonderful visions. The form was decorated with many celestial ornaments and bore many divine upraised weapons. He wore celestial garlands and garments, and many divine scents were smeared over His body. All was wondrous, brilliant, unlimited, all-expanding.

"At that time Arjuna could see in the universal form of the Lord the unlimited expansions of the universe situated in one place although divided into many, many thousands.

The demigods offer prayers to the universal form of the Lord.

"Then, bewildered and astonished, his hair standing on end, Arjuna bowed his head to offer obeisances and with folded hands began to pray to the Supreme Lord."

Arjuna
"My dear Lord Krishna, I see assembled in Your body all the demigods and various other living entities. O Lord of the universe, O universal form, I see in Your body many, many arms, bellies, mouths, and eyes, expanded everywhere, without limit. I see in You no end, no middle, and no beginning. Your form is difficult to see because of its glaring effulgence, spreading on all sides, like blazing fire or the immeasurable radiance of the sun. Yet I see this glowing form everywhere, adorned with various crowns, clubs, and discs.

"You are the supreme primal objective. You are the ultimate resting place of all this universe. You are inexhaustible, and You are the oldest. You are the maintainer of the eternal religion, the Supreme Person. This is my opinion.

"You are without origin, middle, or end. Your glory is unlimited. You have numberless arms, and the sun and moon are Your eyes. I see You with blazing fire coming forth from Your mouth, burning this entire universe by Your own radiance.

"Although You are one, You spread throughout the sky and the planets and all space between. Seeing this wondrous and terrible form, all the planetary systems are perturbed.

"All the hosts of demigods are surrendering before You and entering into You. Some of them, very much afraid, are offering prayers with folded hands. Hosts of great sages and perfected beings, crying 'All peace!' are praying to You by singing the Vedic hymns.

Arjuna sees an unlimited number of faces in the universal form.

"O mighty-armed one, all the planets with their demigods are disturbed at seeing Your great form, with its many faces, eyes, arms, thighs, legs, and Your many terrible teeth; and as they are disturbed, so am I.

"O all-pervading Vishnu, as I gaze upon You with Your radiant colors touching the sky, Your gaping mouths, and Your great glowing eyes, my mind is perturbed by fear. I can no longer maintain my steadiness or equilibrium of mind. O Lord of lords, O refuge of the worlds, please be gracious to me. I cannot keep my balance seeing thus Your blazing deathlike faces and awful teeth. In all directions I am bewildered.

"All the sons of Dhritarastra, along with their allied kings—and our chief soldiers also—are rushing into Your fearful mouths. And some I see trapped with heads smashed between Your teeth. As the many waves of the rivers flow into the ocean, so do all these great warriors enter blazing into Your mouths. I see all people rushing full speed into Your mouths, as moths dash to destruction in a blazing fire.

"O Vishnu, I see You devouring all people from all sides with Your flaming mouths. Covering all the universe with Your effulgence, You are manifest with terrible, scorching rays.

"O Lord of lords, so fierce of form, please tell me who You are. I offer my obeisances unto You; please be gracious to me. You are the primal Lord. I want to know about You, for I do not know Your mission."

The Supreme Lord
"Time I am, the great destroyer of the worlds, and I have come here to destroy all people. With the exception of you [Arjuna and his four brothers], all the soldiers here on both sides will be slain. Therefore get up. Prepare to fight and win glory. Conquer your enemies and enjoy a flourishing kingdom. They are already put to death by My arrangement, and you, O Arjuna, can be but an instrument in the fight. Kill them and do not be disturbed. Simply fight, and you will vanquish your enemies in battle." The whole world moves according to the plan of the Supreme Lord. Those with insufficient knowledge think that nature is moving without a plan and that all manifestations are but accidental

formations. But in fact this cosmic manifestation is a chance for the conditioned souls to go back to God's kingdom, to go back home. Those who follow His plan are victorious in the struggle for existence.

Sanjaya
"O Dhritarastra, after hearing these words from the Supreme Person, the trembling Arjuna offered obeisances with folded hands again and again. He fearfully spoke to Krishna in a faltering voice, as follows."

Arjuna
"O master of the senses, the world becomes joyful upon hearing Your name, and thus everyone becomes attached to You. Although the perfected beings offer You their respectful homage, the demons are afraid, and they flee here and there. All this is rightly done.

"O great one, You are the original creator. Why then should they not offer their respectful obeisances unto You? O limitless one, God of gods, refuge of the universe! You are the invincible source, the cause of all causes, transcendental to this material manifestation.

"You are the original Person, the oldest, the ultimate sanctuary of this manifested cosmic world. You are the knower of everything, and You are all that is knowable. You are the supreme refuge, above the material modes. O limitless form! You pervade this whole cosmic manifestation!

"You are air, and You are the supreme controller! You are fire, You are water, and You are the moon!

"I therefore offer my respectful obeisances unto You a thousand times, and again and yet again! Obeisances to You from the front, from behind, and from all sides! O unbounded power, You are the master of limitless might! You are all-pervading, and thus You are everything!

Arjuna

"Thinking of You as my friend, I have rashly addressed You, 'O Krishna,' 'O my friend,' not knowing Your glories. Please forgive whatever I may have done in madness or in love. I have dishonored You many times, jesting as we relaxed, lay on the same bed, or sat or ate together, sometimes alone and sometimes in front of many friends. O infallible one, please excuse me for all those offenses.

"You are the father of this complete cosmic manifestation, of the moving and the nonmoving. You are its worshipable chief, the supreme spiritual master. No one is equal to You, nor can anyone be one with You. How then could there be anyone greater than You within the three worlds, O Lord of immeasurable power?

"You are the Supreme Lord, to be worshiped by every living being. Thus I fall down to offer You my respectful obeisances and ask Your mercy. As a father tolerates the impudence of his son, or a friend tolerates the impertinence of a friend, or a wife tolerates the familiarity of her partner, please tolerate the wrongs I may have done to You.

"After seeing this universal form, which I have never seen before, I am gladdened, but at the same time my mind is disturbed with fear. Therefore please bestow Your grace upon me and reveal again Your form as the Supreme Person, O Lord of lords, O abode of the universe.

"O universal form, O thousand-armed Lord, I wish to see You in Your four-armed form, with helmeted head and with club, wheel, conch, and lotus flower in Your hands. I long to see You in that form."

The Supreme Person
"My dear Arjuna, happily have I shown you, by My internal potency, this supreme universal form within the material world. No one before you has ever seen this primal form, unlimited and full of glaring effulgence. Not by studying the Vedas, nor by performing sacrifices, nor by charity, nor by pious activities, nor by severe penances can I be seen in this form in the material world.

"You have been perturbed and bewildered by seeing this horrible feature of Mine. Now let it be finished. My devotee, be free again from all disturbances. With a peaceful mind you can now see the form you desire."

Sanjaya
"The Supreme Person, Krishna, displays His real four-armed form and at last shows His two-armed form, thus encouraging the fearful Arjuna."

Arjuna
"O Krishna, seeing this humanlike form, so very beautiful, I am now composed in mind, and I am restored to my original nature."

The Supreme Person
"My dear Arjuna, this form of Mine you are now seeing is very difficult to behold. Even the demigods are ever seeking the opportunity to see this form, which is so dear.

"The form you are seeing with your transcendental eyes cannot be understood simply by studying the *Vedas*, nor by undergoing serious penances, nor by charity, nor by worship. It is not by these means that one can see Me as I am.

"My dear Arjuna, only by undivided devotional service can I be understood as I am, standing before you, and can thus be seen directly. Only in this way can you enter into the mysteries of My understanding." Krishna changes from the universal form to the four-handed form of Narayana and then to His own natural two-handed form. The original two-handed Krishna is the origin of all emanations. Therefore one should conclusively worship the Supreme Lord, Krishna, who has an eternal form of bliss and knowledge. He is the source of all forms of Vishnu, He is the source of all incarnations, and He is the original Supreme Person.

"My dear Arjuna, one who engages in My pure devotional service, free from the contaminations of fruitive activities and mental speculation, one who works for Me, who makes Me the supreme goal of life, and who is friendly to every living being—that person certainly comes to Me."

One can attain success in spiritual activity through devotional service, and to this end one naturally seeks the company of those who are similarly inclined and avoids atheists as well as those who are attracted to fruitive activities and mental speculation.

Yet at the same time, devotees of Krishna are friendly to everyone. Therefore they have no enemy. How is this? Devotees situated in Krishna consciousness know that only devotional service to Krishna can relieve a person from all of life's problems. They have personal experience of this, and therefore they want to introduce this system, Krishna consciousness, into human society. There are many examples in history of the Lord's devotees who

Lord Krishna

risked their lives to spread God consciousness. A familiar example is Jesus Christ. He was crucified by nondevotees, but he sacrificed his life to spread Krishna consciousness. Similarly, in India there are also many examples, such as Thakura Haridasa and Prahlada Maharaja. Why take such risk? Because they were convinced of the value of God consciousness, and wanted to give it to others. Imagine how merciful God is to those engaged in His service, to those who risk everything for Him. Certainly such persons must go to Him after leaving their bodies.

In summary, Krishna has exhibited His universal form (which is a temporary manifestation), His form of time which devours everything, and even His four-handed form of Vishnu. Thus Krishna is the origin of all these manifestations and forms. Those who are attached to the original form of the Lord in love and devotion can see Him always within their hearts.

12

Devotional Service

Arjuna

WHICH ARE CONSIDERED to be more perfect, those who are always properly engaged in Your devotional service or those who worship the impersonal Brahman, the unmanifested?" Those who worship the Supreme Lord directly by engagement in devotional service are called personalists, while those who meditate on the impersonal energy of the Lord, which is beyond the reach of the senses, are called impersonalists.

The Supreme Person
"Those who fix their minds on My personal form and are always engaged in worshiping Me with great and transcendental faith are considered by Me to be most perfect." In answer to Arjuna's question, Krishna clearly says that those who concentrate upon His personal form and worship Him with faith and devotion are most perfect in yoga.

"But those who fully worship the unmanifested, that which lies beyond the perception of the senses, the all-pervading, inconceivable, unchanging, fixed, and immovable—the impersonal conception of the

The three stages of God realization are compared to seeing a hillside from different distances. Realization of the all-pervasive impersonal energy of the Lord (Brahman) is like seeing a misty hill from a great distance. Realization of the localized Supersoul (Paramatma) within the heart of every living entity is like recognizing specific forms on the hillside. And realization of the Supreme Person is like personally meeting the individual who lives on the hill. This is called Bhagavan realization and is the highest.

Absolute Truth—by controlling the various senses and being equally disposed to everyone, such persons, engaged in the welfare of all, at last achieve Me. For those whose minds are attached to the unmanifested, impersonal feature of the Supreme, advancement is very troublesome. To make progress in that discipline is always difficult for those who are embodied." A devotee has no difficulty in approaching the Supreme immediately and directly, whereas the impersonal path to spiritual realization is difficult, with the inherent risk of not realizing the Absolute Truth at the end. Krishna advises against this process. Impersonal realization contradicts the nature of the spiritual, blissful living soul. For every

Krishna compares material existence to an ocean in which the living entities are suffering.

individual living entity the process of Krishna consciousness, which entails full engagement in devotional service, is the best and surest path. If one chooses to ignore devotional service, there is an intrinsic danger of turning to atheism. The personalist, without any risk, trouble, or difficulty, approaches the Supreme Person directly.

"But those who worship Me, giving up all their activities unto Me and being devoted to Me without deviation, engaged in devotional service and always meditating upon Me, having fixed their minds upon Me, O Arjuna—for them I am the swift deliverer from the ocean of birth and death." It does not matter in what kind of work we engage, but we should do that work only as an offering to Krishna. The process is very simple: we can devote ourselves to Krishna in our occupations and at the same time engage in chanting Hare Krishna, Hare Krishna, Krishna

A letter in a mailbox authorized by the post office will go to its destination, while a letter in some homemade box will not go anywhere. Similarly, worship of a form of the Lord authorized in scripture is received by the Lord; worship of an imaginary, inauthentic form goes nowhere.

Krishna, Hare Hare / Hare Rama, Hare Rama, Rama Rama, Hare Hare. The Supreme Lord promises that without delay He will deliver a pure devotee thus engaged from the cycle of birth, death, and rebirth.

"Just fix your mind upon Me, the Supreme Person, and engage all your intelligence in Me. Thus you will live in Me always, without a doubt.

"My dear Arjuna, if you cannot fix your mind upon Me without deviation, then follow the regulative principles of *bhakti-yoga*. In this way develop a desire to attain Me." Love of God exists in a dormant state in everyone's heart. This love manifests in different ways, but it is contaminated by material association. However, through regulative principles, we can purify our hearts of this material association and revive our dormant love for Krishna. That is the process of *bhakti-yoga*.

To practice the regulative principles of *bhakti-yoga* we should, under the guidance of an expert spiritual master, follow certain principles: we should rise early in the morning, take a bath, enter the temple (which can be in the home), offer prayers and chant the Lord's holy names, take food that has been offered to the Lord, and hear or read the *Bhagavad-gita As It Is*. These practices help us rise to the level of love of God and then progress into the spiritual kingdom of God.

"If you cannot practice the regulations of *bhakti-yoga*, then just try to work for Me, because by working for Me you will come to the perfect stage." If we cannot directly practice the regulative principles of *bhakti-yoga*, we can try to help those who are propagating *bhakti-yoga*.

"If, however, you are unable to work in this consciousness of Me, then try to act giving up all results of your work and try to be self-situated." It may be that a person is unable even to sympathize with the activities of Krishna consciousness because of social, family, or religious considerations. Krishna advises that such persons give in charity or serve some good cause. Thus they may be gradually elevated to the state of knowledge. By giving in charity to a hospital or to some other social institution, or by performing community or national service, we may purify our minds of material desires and illusions and, in that purified state, gradually come to understand God. Of course, awareness of God is not dependent on any other experience, because this awareness in and of itself can purify the mind, but if impediments still remain in accepting God consciousness, then we may choose to give up the results of our actions as an indirect offering to God.

"If you cannot take to this practice, then engage yourself in the cultivation of knowledge. Better than knowledge, however, is meditation, and better than meditation is renunciation of the fruits of action, for by such renunciation one can attain peace of mind." To reach the Supreme Lord, the highest goal, there are two processes: the direct path and gradual development. The direct path of loving devotional service is not possible for everyone; therefore the indirect process—renunciation of the fruits of one's activities, followed by the stages of knowledge, meditation, and realization of Brahman and the Supersoul—is also good. But the *Bhagavad-gita* emphasizes the direct method.

"One who is not envious but is a kind friend to all living entities, who does not think of oneself as a proprietor and who is free from false ego, who is equal in both happiness and distress, who is tolerant, always satisfied, self-controlled, and engaged in devotional service with determination, with mind and intelligence fixed on Me—such a devotee of Mine is very dear to Me." Such a standard of devotional service is undoubtedly

Some philosophers propose that the material creation is false, but this is not supported by the Bhagavad-gita. Just as a meal is real, although temporary, so is the material creation.

very rare, but a devotee becomes situated in that stage by following the regulative principles of devotional service.

"One for whom no one is put into difficulty and who is not disturbed by anyone, who is equipoised in happiness and distress, fear and anxiety, is very dear to Me.

"My devotee who is not dependent on the ordinary course of activities, who is pure, expert, without cares, free from all pains, and not striving for some result, is very dear to Me.

"One who neither rejoices nor grieves, who neither laments nor desires, and who renounces both auspicious and inauspicious things—such a devotee is very dear to Me.

"One who is equal to friends and enemies, who is equipoised in honor and dishonor, heat and cold, happiness and distress, fame and infamy, who is always free from contaminating association, always silent and satisfied with anything, who doesn't care for any residence, who is fixed in knowledge, and who is engaged in devotional service—such a person is very dear to Me." Devotees do not extraneously endeavor to acquire these qualifications, but engagement in Krishna consciousness and devotional service automatically helps devotees develop them.

"Those who follow this imperishable path of devotional service and who completely engage themselves with faith, making Me the supreme goal, are very, very dear to Me." The question of who is better—one who is engaged in the path of impersonal Brahman or one who is engaged in the personal service of the Supreme Lord—was raised by Arjuna, and the Lord replies so explicitly that there is no doubt that devotional service to the Lord is the best of all processes of spiritual realization. As long as we do not have the chance to associate with a pure devotee, the impersonal conception may be beneficial. But by hearing from or reading the words of a pure devotee, we develop directly a desire to engage in Krishna consciousness in pure devotional service, and this devotional service is the path for self-realization.

Trees are an emblem of tolerance, for they silently endure all inconveniences and yet continue to offer their soothing shelter to all.

13

Nature, the Enjoyer and Consciousness

STARTING WITH CHAPTER THIRTEEN, Krishna explains how the living entity comes into contact with material nature, how it is delivered, and how, although the living entity is completely different from the material body, it somehow becomes related.

Arjuna
"O my dear Krishna, I wish to know about nature, the enjoyer, and the field and the knower of the field, and of knowledge and the object of knowledge."

The Supreme Person
"This body, O Arjuna, is called the field, and one who knows this body is called the knower of the field. You should understand that I am also the knower in all bodies, and to understand this body and its knower is called knowledge. That is My opinion." Here Lord Krishna presents three different topics of study: the Lord, the living entity, and matter. In every field of activity, in every body, exist two souls: the individual soul and the Supersoul, the Supreme Lord. We may be the knower of our own body, but we are not in knowledge of other bodies. The Supreme Lord, who is present as the Supersoul in all bodies, knows everything about all bodies. He knows all the different bodies of all the various species of life.

Krishna compares the body to a field and the soul to the field's owner. The products of the field depend upon the desires of the owner.

The Lord then explains that twenty items constitute knowledge. "Humility; pridelessness; nonviolence; tolerance; simplicity; approaching a bona fide spiritual master; cleanliness; steadiness; self-control; renunciation of the objects of sense gratification; absence of false ego; the perception of the evil of birth, death, old age, and disease; detachment; freedom from entanglement with children, spouse, home, and the rest; even-mindedness amid pleasant and unpleasant events; constant and unalloyed devotion to Me; aspiring to live in a solitary place; detachment from the general mass of people; accepting the importance of self-realization; and philosophical search for the Absolute Truth—all these I declare to be knowledge, and besides this, whatever there may be is ignorance."

Of all these descriptions of the process of knowledge, the most important point is unalloyed devotional service to the Lord. If we do not approach the transcendental service of the Lord, then the other nineteen items mentioned here are of no particular value. In this regard, the principle of accepting a spiritual master is essential. Even if we take to devotional service, it is most important. Transcendental life begins when we accept a bona fide spiritual master. Then, beginning from humility, we gradually reawaken our spiritual knowledge, realize that we are subordinate to the Supreme Lord and that, due to rebelling against Him, we have become subordinate to material nature. We come to know and be convinced of these truths.

"I shall now explain the knowable, knowing which you will taste the eternal. The individual soul is beginningless and subordinate to Me, and lies beyond the cause and effect of this material world.

"The Supersoul pervades everything: everywhere are His hands and legs, His eyes, heads, and faces, and He has ears everywhere. The Supersoul is the original source of all senses, yet He is without material senses. He is unattached, although He is the maintainer of all living beings. He transcends the modes of nature, and at the same time He is the master of all the modes of material nature."

The Supreme is different from the individual soul. The Supreme Lord can extend His hand without limit; the individual soul cannot. The Supreme Lord's senses are transcendental; they are not materially covered, as the individual soul's are. With our material senses we cannot see or understand Him, but when we purify our senses and minds by practicing Krishna consciousness, we can see Him constantly.

"The Supreme Truth exists outside and inside of all living beings, the moving and the nonmoving. Because He is subtle, He is beyond the power of the material senses to see or to know. Although far, far away, He is also near to all.

"Although the Supersoul appears to be divided among all beings, He is never divided. He is situated as one. He is the source of light in all luminous objects. He is beyond the darkness of matter and is unmanifested. He is knowledge, He is the object of knowledge, and He is the goal of knowledge. He is situated in everyone's heart."

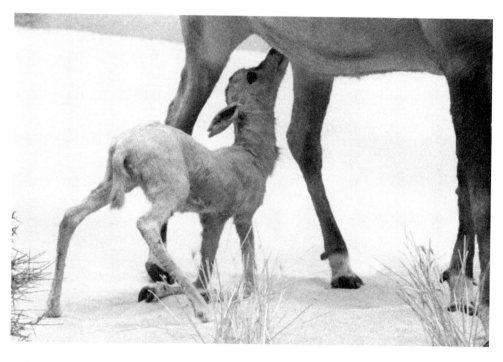

What is commonly called "instinct" is the direction of the Supersoul— God in the heart of every living being.

Thus Krishna has described the field of activity (the body), the process of understanding, and both the soul and the Supersoul. "Only My devotees can understand this thoroughly and thus attain My nature."

The body is the field of activity and is composed of material nature. The individual living entity (the soul) is embodied and enjoys the activities of the body. The living entity is one knower, and the Supersoul is the other. Both the individual living entity and the Supersoul are different manifestations of the Supreme Lord. The living entity is His energy, and the Supersoul is His personal expansion.

"Nature is said to be the cause of all material causes and effects, whereas the living entity is the cause of the various sufferings and enjoyments in this world. The living entities in material nature thus follow the ways of life, enjoying the three modes of material nature. This is due to their association with that material nature. Thus they meet with good and evil amongst various species."

According to our desires and activities, material nature places us in certain bodies, or residential quarters. Material happiness and distress are due to our bodies, and not to ourselves as we are. In our original state there is no doubt of eternal pleasure; that is our real state.

As long as we are attached to material existence, we have to continue transmigrating from one body to another. Under the influence of material desire, we are born sometimes as demigods, sometimes as humans, sometimes as beasts, as birds, as worms, as aquatics, as saintly persons, or as bugs. This is going on due to our material desires and our association with the different modes of nature.

"Yet in this body there is another, a transcendental enjoyer, who is the Lord, the supreme proprietor, who exists as the overseer

As the sun simultaneously appears in many water pots, yet remains one, the Supreme Lord resides within every body, beside the living being, yet He remains the one Supreme Person.

and permitter, and who is known as the Supersoul." The Lord is always eager to bring the living entities back to the spiritual kingdom, but with our minute independence we continually reject this invitation. This misuse of independence is the cause of our material suffering.

"Those who understand this philosophy concerning material nature, the living entity, and the interaction of the modes of nature are sure to attain liberation. Such persons will not take birth here again, regardless of their present position.

"There are those who, although not conversant in spiritual knowledge, begin to worship the Supreme Person upon hearing about Him from others. Because of their tendency to hear from authorities, they also transcend the path of birth and death." We do not need to change our

The conditioned soul is helplessly kicked from one body to another, just as a soccer ball is kicked on the playing field.

position or occupation to understand God, however we cannot understand Him through speculative reasoning. Faithful hearing from a self-realized person will help us transcend this material existence and go back to God's abode, back to home.

"O Arjuna, know that whatever you see in existence, both the moving and the nonmoving, is only a combination of the field of activities and the knower of the field.

"One who sees the Supersoul accompanying the individual soul in all bodies, and who understands that neither the soul nor the Supersoul within the destructible body is ever destroyed, actually sees." After the destruction of the body, both the soul and the Supersoul exist, and they continue eternally in various moving and nonmoving forms.

"Those who see the Supersoul equally present everywhere, in every living being, do not degrade themselves by their minds. Thus they approach the transcendental destination." Our minds are generally addicted to the endless process of sense gratification; but when we turn our minds to the Supersoul, we become advanced in spiritual understanding.

"Those who see that all activities are performed by the body, which is created of material nature, and see that the self does nothing, actually see." We are forced to act—either for happiness or distress—by our bodily constitutions. The self, however, is outside all these bodily activities.

According to our past desires, we are given our bodies to fulfill those desires. Practically speaking, bodies are machines designed by the Supreme Lord to fulfill desires. Because of desires, we embrace the difficult circumstances of material life to suffer or enjoy. When we develop this transcendental perception, we can distinguish ourselves from bodily activities and become actual seers.

"When sensible persons cease to see different identities due to different material bodies and they see how living entities are expanded everywhere, they attain the Brahman conception." When we can see that the various bodies of living entities arise due to the different desires of each individual soul and that the body does not actually belong to the soul itself, we actually see.

With the body, we acquire senses which are drawn to certain sense objects. Thus a hog sees stool as a palatable meal.

"Those with the vision of eternity can see that the imperishable soul is transcendental, eternal, and beyond the modes of nature. Despite contact with the material body, O Arjuna, the soul neither does anything nor is entangled." We appear to be born with the birth of our material bodies, but actually we are eternal; we are not born, and in spite of our being situated within material bodies, we are transcendental to them. Thus we cannot be destroyed. By nature we are full of bliss. We do not engage ourselves in any material activities; therefore the activities performed due to our contact with material bodies do not entangle us.

"The sky, due to its subtle nature, does not mix with anything, although it is all-pervading. Similarly, the soul does not mix with the body, though situated in that body." Air enters into water, mud, stool, and whatever else is present; still it does not mix with anything. Similarly, the living entity, even though situated in varieties of bodies, is aloof from them due to its subtle nature. Therefore it is impossible to see with material eyes how one is in contact with the body and how one leaves the body after its destruction. No one in science can ascertain this.

"O Arjuna, as the sun alone illuminates all this universe, so does the living entity, one within the body, illuminate the entire body by consciousness.

"Those who see with eyes of knowledge the difference between the body and the knower of the body, and who can also understand the process of liberation from bondage in material nature, attain to the supreme goal." This body is a gross manifestation of matter; the subtle manifestations are the mind and its psychological effects. But above this, there is the soul, and there is also the Supersoul. The soul and the Supersoul are two. When we can see the constitution of the whole material manifestation as this combination of the soul and material elements, and when we can also see the situation of the Supreme Soul, we become eligible for transfer to the spiritual world. We are meant to contemplate and realize these things, and we can have a complete understanding of this chapter with the help of a self-realized spiritual master.

The soul and the Supersoul within the body
resemble two birds sitting as friends in a tree.
The conditioned soul tries to enjoy the fruits of
the body, while the Supersoul simply watches,
waiting for His friend to turn to Him.

The symptoms of
the mode of
passion are great
attachment and
unlimited desires
and longings.
Passion typically
governs the
relationship
between a man
and a woman.

14

The Three Modes of Material Nature

I N THE PREVIOUS CHAPTER, we understood that knowledge frees us from
material entanglement and that association with the modes of nature
entangles us in this material world. Now, in this chapter, the
Supreme Lord explains what those modes of nature are, how they act,
how they bind, and how they liberate. One who understands this chapter
will attain perfection.

The Supreme Lord
"Again I shall declare to you this supreme wisdom, the best of all knowledge, knowing which all the sages have attained the supreme perfection.
By becoming fixed in this knowledge, one can attain to the transcendental nature like My own. Thus established, one is not born at the time of
creation or disturbed at the time of dissolution."

After acquiring perfect transcendental knowledge, devotees acquire
qualitative equality with the Supreme Lord, becoming free from the rep-
etition of birth and death. Devotees do not, however, lose their identities
as individual souls. Such liberated souls reach the transcendental planets
of the spiritual sky and there continue to engage in the Lord's transcendental loving service. There they have spiritual forms, engage in spiritual
activities, and experience spiritual relationships.

"The total material substance is the source of birth, and it is that substance that I impregnate, making possible the births of all living beings,
O Arjuna." The Supreme Lord Himself makes the combination of material nature and the living entity possible. Material nature is not the cause

of the birth of the living entities. The Supreme Lord gives the seed, and the living entities only appear to be products of material nature. Thus, every living entity, according to its past activities, receives and inhabits a different body, created by material nature, to enjoy or suffer according to its past deeds.

"Understand that all species of life are made possible by birth in this material nature, and that I am the seed-giving father." The Supreme Lord is the original father of all living entities. Material nature, which provides the bodies of all living entities, is the mother. Thus the material world is impregnated by the Lord with living entities, who appear in various forms at the time of creation according to their past deeds.

"Material nature consists of three modes—goodness, passion, and ignorance. When the eternal living entity comes in contact with nature, O mighty-armed Arjuna, it becomes conditioned by these modes."

People used to believe that scorpions were born of rice. Now we know that scorpions grow from eggs laid in the rice. Similarly, material nature is not the cause of birth for the living entities. Living beings appear to be products of matter, but in truth the Supreme Lord is the seed-giving father.

The living entity, because it is transcendental, has nothing to do with this material world. Still, because it has become conditioned by material world, it must act under the spell of the three modes of material nature. This is the cause of the varieties of happiness and distress.

"O sinless one, the mode of goodness, being purer than the others, is illuminating, and it frees one from all sinful reactions. Those situated in that mode become conditioned by a sense of happiness and knowledge.

"The mode of passion is born of unlimited desires and longings, and because of this the embodied living entity is bound to material fruitive actions.

"O Arjuna, know that the mode of darkness, born of ignorance, is the delusion of all embodied living entities. The results of this mode are madness, indolence, and sleep, which bind the conditioned soul.

"O Arjuna, the mode of goodness conditions one to happiness; passion conditions one to fruitive action; and ignorance, covering one's knowledge, binds one to madness.

"Sometimes the mode of goodness becomes prominent, defeating the modes of passion and ignorance. Sometimes the mode of passion defeats goodness and ignorance, and at other times ignorance defeats goodness and passion. In this way there is always competition for supremacy."

The characteristics of a specific mode of nature are in our activities, in eating, working, recreation, and so forth. By the quality of our activities, we can understand in what mode of nature we are situated.

"The manifestation of the mode of goodness can be experienced when one is illuminated by knowledge. O Arjuna, when there is an increase in the mode of passion, the symptoms of great attachment, fruitive activity, intense endeavor, uncontrollable desire, and hankering develop. When there is an increase in the mode of ignorance, darkness, inertia, madness, and illusion manifest.

"When one dies in the mode of goodness, one attains to the pure higher planets of the great sages. When one dies in the mode of passion, one takes birth among those engaged in fruitive activities; and when one dies in the mode of ignorance, one takes birth in the animal kingdom." There is no guarantee that a human will again attain the human status.

"The result of pious action is pure and is said to be in the mode of goodness. But action done in the mode of passion results in misery, and action performed in the mode of ignorance results in foolishness.

"From the mode of goodness, real knowledge develops; from the mode of passion, greed develops; and from the mode of ignorance develop foolishness, madness, and illusion." In the mode of passion, people become greedy, and their hankering for sense enjoyment has no limit. Adequate money and arrangements for sense gratification guarantee neither happiness nor peace of mind. Engaged in the mode of passion, people become unhappy, and their professions and occupations are troublesome. They have to devise schemes to acquire enough money to maintain their positions, and this ultimately produces misery. In the mode of ignorance, people become mad. Being distressed by their circumstances, they take shelter of intoxication, and thus they sink more deeply into ignorance.

"Those situated in the mode of goodness gradually go upward to the higher planets; those in passion live on the earthly planets; and those in the abominable mode of ignorance go down to the hellish worlds.

"When one properly sees that in all activities no performer is at work other than these modes of nature and one knows the Supreme Lord, who is transcendental to all these modes, one attains My spiritual nature."

Through the instruction of a bona fide spiritual master, one can comprehend one's spiritual position, one's material body, one's senses, how one is entrapped, and how one is under the spell of the material modes of nature. Controlled by these modes, one is helpless, but when one can perceive one's true identity as spirit soul, then one can attain the transcendental platform. Actually, the living entity is not the performer of different activities. Being situated in a particular body determined by a

A vulture flies high in the sky, but merely in search of a carcass. Similarly, we attain the exalted human birth, but, influenced by the modes of nature, we seek happiness in matter instead of spirit.

particular mode of nature, it is forced to act. But for one who is able to see things as they are, the influence of material nature gradually ceases.

"When one is able to transcend these three modes associated with the material body, one can become free from birth, death, old age, and their distresses and can enjoy nectar even in this life."

Arjuna
"O my dear Lord, by which symptoms is one known who is transcendental to these three modes? What is one's behavior? And how does one transcend the modes of nature?"

The Supreme Person
"O son of Pandu, one who does not hate illumination, attachment, and delusion when they are present or long for them when they disappear; who is unwavering and undisturbed through all these reactions of the material qualities, remaining neutral and transcendental, knowing that the modes alone are active; who is situated in the self and regards as alike happiness and distress; who looks upon a lump of earth, a stone, and a piece of gold with an equal eye; who is equal toward the desirable and the undesirable; who is steady, situated equally well in praise and blame, honor and dishonor; who treats alike both friend and enemy; and who has renounced all material activities—such a person has transcended the modes of nature."

Arjuna has asked three questions, and the Lord answers them one after another.

As far as the symptoms of those who are transcendentally situated, the Lord states that such persons have no envy and do not hanker for anything. Those who engage in the devotional service of the Lord soon transcend their identification with the material body. In material consciousness, we act only for sense gratification, or for the pleasure of the body, but when we transfer consciousness to Krishna, sense gratification automatically stops. We do not need these material bodies, nor do we need to accept their dictates. The material modes of nature will act on the body, but as spirit soul the self is aloof from such demands.

Krishna says that there is no being, either here or in the higher planetary systems, who is free from the influence of the three modes of material nature. Attachment to the body is one of the symptoms of a person so influenced.

How do we become aloof? We desire neither to enjoy the body, nor to be free of it. Thus transcendentally situated, the devotees become automatically free of the influence of material illusion. They see everything equally because they know perfectly well that they have nothing to do with material existence. As far as the behavior of transcendentally situated persons, they perform their duties in God consciousness and do not mind whether people honor or dishonor them. Social and political issues are temporary upheavals and disturbances and do not affect them. They can attempt anything for the Lord, but for their personal gain they attempt nothing.

In answer to Arjuna's third question, "How does one transcend the modes of nature?" the Lord replies, "One who engages in full devotional service, unfailing in all circumstances, at once transcends the modes of material nature and thus comes to the level of impersonal realization [Brahman]. And I am the basis of the impersonal Brahman, which is immortal, imperishable, and eternal and is the constitutional position of ultimate happiness."

The transcendental position is *bhakti-yoga*—always acting for God. If we engage ourselves in the service of God with unfailing determination, then, although these modes of material nature are very powerful, we can overcome them easily.

Bhakti-yoga involves the Lord, the devotee, and the active exchange of love between the Lord and the devotee. Without the presence of two— the Supreme Soul and the individual soul—*bhakti-yoga* has no meaning.

The attainment of the Brahman conception of life is the first stage in self-realization. At this stage the Brahman-realized person is transcendental to the material position, but such a person is not actually perfect even in Brahman realization. If one wants, one can gradually rise to the position of realization of Supersoul within and then to the realization of the Supreme Person.

The living entities, although transcendental by nature, desire to enjoy the material world, and due to this desire, they fall under the influence of the three material modes of nature and the illusion of bodily identification. In their constitutional position, living entities are above the three modes of material nature, but they become entangled by association with material nature. Due to this association, the living entities mistakenly think they can dominate and enjoy the material world. But, by engagement in devotional service in full Krishna consciousness, they can be rid of these illusory and unlawful desires and again be situated in their original, transcendental position.

A chart of the many aspects of the three modes of material nature, as described by Krishna in Chapters 14, 17, and 18 of the *Bhagavad-gita*, appears on pages 150–153.

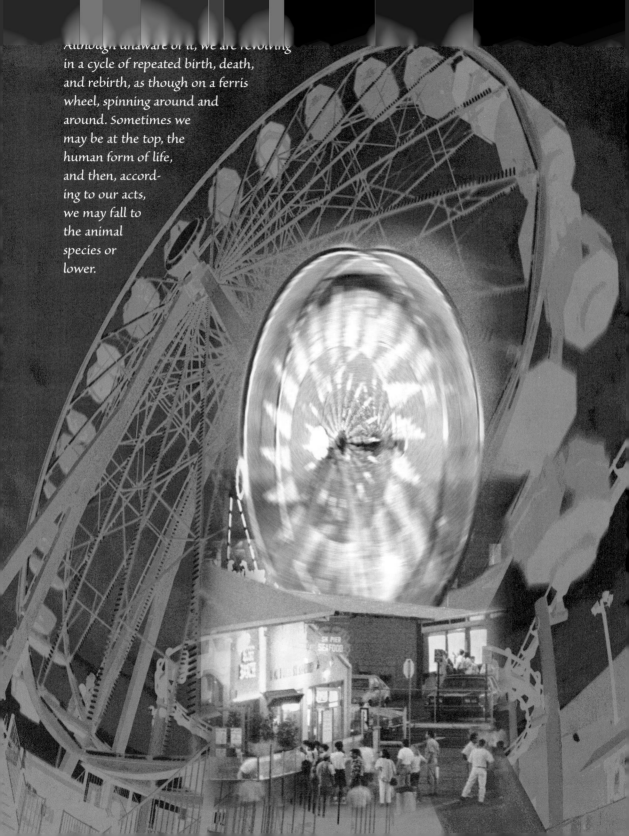

Although unaware of it, we are revolving in a cycle of repeated birth, death, and rebirth, as though on a ferris wheel, spinning around and around. Sometimes we may be at the top, the human form of life, and then, according to our acts, we may fall to the animal species or lower.

	Ignorance	Passion	Goodness	Pure Goodness*
General Characteristics	Foolishness, madness, illusion, inertia, indolence, and sleep	Unlimited, uncontrollable desires and longings; intense endeavor; greed, bondage to material fruitive activities, and attachment to the fruits of action	Relative purity, illumination, happiness, and freedom from sinful reactions; conducive to real knowledge	Complete, unmotivated, unfailing devotion to the Supreme Person; absolute knowledge, purity, illumination, happiness, and freedom from sinful reaction
Destination After Death	The hellish worlds and the animal kingdom	The association of fruitive workers on the earthly planets	The heavenly planets	The eternal abode of the Supreme Lord
Objects of Worship	Ghosts and spirits	Demons, powerful people, and self-proclaimed, imitation gods	The demigods and the impersonal conception of God	The Supreme Lord
Food	Tasteless, stale, putrid, decomposed, unclean; prepared more than three hours before being eaten; remnants of the meals of others; meat, fish, eggs, and liquor	Too bitter, sour, salty, pungent, rich, dry, or hot; causes pain, distress, and disease	Increases longevity, purifies one's existence, gives strength, health, happiness, and satisfaction; nourishing, sweet, juicy, fattening, and palatable; milk products, grains, sugar, fruits, and vegetables	Frees one from past sinful reactions and protects one from future contamination; invokes one's dormant Krishna consciousness; prepared by devotees according to scriptural injunctions and offered with devotion to the Supreme Lord; remnants of the meal of a saintly person
Sacrifice	Performed faithlessly, contrary to scriptural	Performed proudly, ostentatiously, for the	Performed as a duty, according to scriptural regu-	Performed according to scriptural injunctions, and

	Transcendental	Goodness	Passion	Ignorance
	...under the guidance of the spiritual master, to please the Supreme Lord	...lations, and with no expectation of reward	...sake of some material end or benefit (such as elevation to the heavenly kingdom)	...injunctions, and with no spiritual food distributed, no hymns chanted, and no remunerations to the priests
Austerity	Performed with faith and with a desire to satisfy the Supreme Personality of Godhead	Performed with faith and without desires for one's material benefit. *Bodily Austerities:* cleanliness, simplicity, celibacy, nonviolence, offering of respect to the demigods, *brahmanas,* spiritual master, and superiors like the mother and father. *Austerities of Speech:* speaking beneficially, truthfully, inoffensively, and with reference to Vedic authorities. *Mental Austerities:* serenity, simplicity, gravity, self-control, purity of thought, and detachment from sense gratification	Performed ostentatiously to gain respect, honor, and reverence; brings only unstable, temporary results	Performed foolishly by means of obstinate self-torture or to destroy or injure others
Charity	Performed only to satisfy the Supreme Lord	Performed as a duty, at the proper time and place, to a worthy person and with no expectation of material returns	Performed to get something in return, with a desire for fruitive results, or in a begrudging mood	Performed at an improper time and place, to an unworthy person (like a drunkard), or contemptuously, without respect

	Ignorance	Passion	Goodness	Pure Goodness*
Renunciation	Consists of giving up one's prescribed duties because of illusion	Consists of giving up one's prescribed duties because of fear or because they appear troublesome	Consists of performing one's prescribed duties because they ought to be done and abandoning attachment to the fruits of one's work	Consists of performing one's prescribed duties in Krishna consciousness and employing the fruits of one's work for the satisfaction of Krishna
Knowledge	Very meager; unrelated to the Absolute Truth; breeds attachment to one kind of work as the be-all and end-all; concerned only with bodily comforts, eating, sleeping, mating and defending, and thus resembles the knowledge of animals	Gives rise to speculative doctrines and theories through which one sees the body as the self and consciousness as a temporary by-product of the body; rules out the existence of the eternal, individual soul within	Gives rise to a vision of one undivided spiritual force within the bodies of all living beings (the impersonal conception)	Enables one to see all living beings as eternal, spiritual individual, spiritual servants of the supreme living being, Krishna
Action	Irresponsible, violent, distressing to others; performed in illusion, without consideration of scriptural injunctions or future bondage and consequences; results in further foolishness	Performed under false egoism and with great effort, to satisfy one's desires to enjoy the fruits of one's work; results in distress	Performed under scriptural regulations, as a matter of duty, without attachment, and without love and hate, by one who renounces the fruits of one's actions; results in purification	Performed solely for the satisfaction of Krishna and the spiritual master
Worker	Disregards scriptural injunctions;	Attached to the fruits of one's work and	Free from material attachments, pride, and false	Unconditionally serves Krishna and the spiritual

(master under any and all circumstances)	(ego;) enthusiastic, resolute, and unswayed by success or failure	intent upon enjoying them; greedy, envious, unclean; entangled by happiness when successful and distress when unsuccessful	materialistic, obstinate, cheating, lazy, morose, procrastinating, and expert in insulting others
Understanding Always perfectly considers Krishna through personal realization, confirmed by the scriptures and the spiritual master	Intelligently discriminates, under scriptural direction, between what is to be done and not to be done, what is to be feared and what not to be feared, and what is liberating and what is binding	Misguided, perverse, and imperfect; cannot distinguish between religion and irreligion, truth and untruth, and what should and should not be done	Considers irreligion to be religion, and religion to be irreligion; strives always in the wrong direction
Determination Fully engaged in Krishna consciousness and never deviated by anything else	Practically unbreakable; sustained with steadfastness by yoga, which controls the activities of the mind, life, and senses	Fixed upon securing the fruits of religion, economic development, and sense gratification	Cannot go beyond daydreaming, fearfulness, lamentation, moroseness, and illusion
Happiness Derived from service rendered by a purified soul to the Supreme Person in an eternal loving relationship; ever-increasing ecstasy; unparalleled by any mundane experience or emotion	Compared to poison in the beginning, but nectar in the end, because it involves control of the mind and senses and awakens one to self-realization	Derived from contact of the senses with their objects; seems like nectar at first, but poison at the end; epitomized by sexual enjoyment	Blind to self-realization; delusion from beginning to end; comes about from sleep, laziness, and illusion

Pure goodness is fully spiritual and is transcendental to the three modes of material nature.

15

The Yoga of the Supreme Person

THIS CHAPTER EXPLAINS that the purpose of Vedic study is to understand Krishna. Therefore one who is Krishna conscious, who is engaged in devotional service, has realized the conclusion of the *Vedas*. The first five verses describe the process of freeing oneself from the attachment to and the possession of matter. The rest of the chapter discusses the highest yoga, the yoga of the Supreme Person.

The Supreme Lord
"It is said that there is an imperishable banyan tree that has its roots upward and its branches downward and whose leaves are the Vedic hymns. One who knows this tree is the knower of the *Vedas*. The branches of this tree extend downward and upward, nourished by the three modes of material nature. The twigs are the objects of the senses. This tree also has roots going down, and these are bound to the fruitive actions of human society."

In previous chapters Krishna has explained many processes for freeing ourselves from material entanglement, and He has declared that the best of all those processes is devotional service to the Supreme Lord. The basic principle of devotional service is detachment from material activities and attachment to the transcendental service of the Lord.

Krishna compares the spiritual world
to a tree and this material world to
the tree's reflection. This world is a
replica of the spiritual world, but
perverted. What's here is also there,
but there it's eternal and real.

"The real form of this tree cannot be perceived in this world. No one can understand where it ends, where it begins, or where its foundation is. But with determination one must cut down this strongly rooted tree with the weapon of detachment. Thereafter, one must seek that place from which, having gone, one never returns, and there surrender to that Supreme Person from whom everything began and from whom everything has extended since time immemorial.

"Those who are free from false prestige, illusion, and false association, who understand the eternal, who are done with material lust, who are freed from the dualities of happiness and distress, and who, unbewildered, know how to surrender unto the Supreme Person attain to that eternal kingdom."

For those who are always expecting some honor in this material world, it is not possible to surrender to the Supreme Person. Only when one is free from delusion caused by pride can one begin the process of surrender. Pride is due to illusion, for although people come here, stay for a brief time and then go away, they have the foolish notion that they are the lords of this world. The whole world moves under this impression. People consider the land, this earth, to belong to human society, and they have divided the land under the false impression that they are the proprietors. Such false conceptions bind them to the material world. When we understand things as they really are, we can understand what is our own and what is not actually our own. We become full in knowledge, and only then is it possible to surrender to the Supreme Lord.

"That supreme abode of Mine is not illumined by the sun or moon, nor by fire or electricity. Those who reach it never return to this material world."

We should be captivated by this information. We should desire to extricate ourselves from this false reflection of reality and transfer ourselves to that eternal world. If we are too attached to this material world, it is difficult to cut that attachment, but if we take to God consciousness, then gradually we become detached, surrender to the Lord, and achieve His supreme abode.

"The living entities in this conditioned world are My eternal fragmental parts. Due to conditioned life, they are struggling very hard with the six senses, which include the mind."

As eternal, fragmental parts and parcels of the Supreme Lord, the living entities also have fragmental portions of His qualities, one of which is independence. Every living entity, as an individual soul, has its own personal individuality and minute independence. By misusing that independence, one becomes a conditioned soul dominated by the material modes of nature; by proper use of independence, one is liberated—freed from this material condition of existence and engaged in transcendental loving service to the Lord.

"The living entity in the material world carries different conceptions of life from one body to another as the air carries aromas. Thus the living entity takes one kind of body and again quits it to take another." The living entity itself determines its next body. At the time of death, the consciousness one has created will carry one to the next type of body. One's subtle body, which carries the conception of one's next physical body, develops that body in the next life.

"The living entity, thus taking another gross body, obtains a certain type of ear, eye, tongue, nose, and sense of touch, which are grouped about the mind. The living entity thus enjoys a particular set of sense objects.

"The foolish cannot understand how a living entity can quit its body, nor can they understand what sort of body it enjoys under the spell of the modes of nature. But one whose eyes are trained in knowledge can see all this." One who is fooled by lust and desire loses all power to understand the stay in a particular body and the ensuing change of body. One who has developed spiritual knowledge, however, can see that the spirit is different from the body, is changing its body, and is enjoying in different ways.

A soul that enters the body of a dog is forced to make the sounds and movements of a dog's body; the dog's body does not allow the soul to act otherwise.

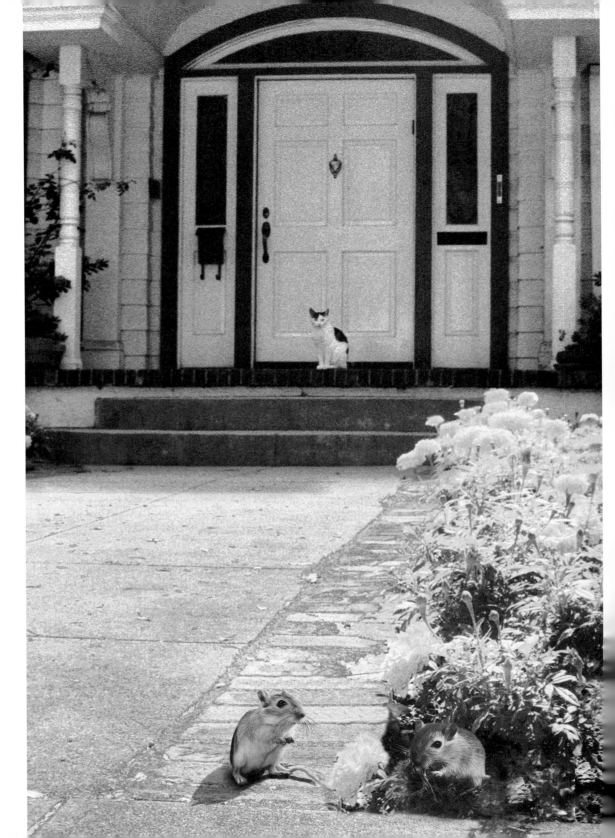

"The endeavoring transcendentalists, who are situated in self-realization, can see all this clearly. But those whose minds are not developed and who are not situated in self-realization cannot see what is taking place, though they may try.

"The splendor of the sun, which dissipates the darkness of this world, comes from Me. And the splendor of the moon and the splendor of fire are also from Me. I enter into each planet, and by My energy they stay in orbit. I become the moon and thereby supply the juice of life to all vegetables. I am the fire of digestion in the bodies of all living entities.

"I am seated in everyone's heart, and from Me come remembrance, knowledge, and forgetfulness. By all the *Vedas* I am to be known. Indeed I am the compiler of *Vedanta*, and I am the knower of the *Vedas*." The Supreme Lord is so complete that, for the deliverance of the conditioned souls, He is the supplier and digester of their food, the witness of their activities, the giver of knowledge in the form of the *Vedas*, and, as the Supreme Person, Lord Krishna, the teacher of the *Bhagavad-gita*.

"There are two classes of beings, the fallible and the infallible. In the material world every living entity is fallible, and in the spiritual world every living entity is called infallible.

"Besides these two, there is the greatest living personality, the Supreme Soul, the imperishable Lord Himself, who has entered the three worlds and is maintaining them.

"Because I am transcendental, beyond both the fallible and the infallible, and because I am the greatest, I am celebrated both in the world and in the *Vedas* as that Supreme Person. Those who know Me as the Supreme Lord, without doubting, are the knowers of everything. They therefore engage themselves in full devotional service to Me, O Arjuna. This is the most confidential part of the Vedic scriptures, O sinless one, and I now disclose it. Those who understand this will become wise, and their endeavors will know perfection."

By understanding this philosophy of the Supreme Lord and engaging in His transcendental service, we are freed from all contaminations of

If a person who is greatly attached to his house dies thinking of it, he may again take birth in the same house, although perhaps not as a human being.

the modes of material nature. Wherever unalloyed, uninterrupted devotional service exists, the material contamination cannot co-exist. Devotional service to the Lord and the Lord Himself are the same, because they are spiritual; devotional service takes place within the internal (spiritual) energy of the Supreme Lord. The Lord is like the sun, and ignorance is like darkness. Where the sun is present, there is no question of darkness. Therefore, whenever devotional service is present under the proper guidance of a bona fide spiritual master, there is no question of ignorance.

The sun evaporates ocean water to form a cloud, which then prevents us from seeing the sun. Likewise God creates the illusion which prevents materialists from seeing Him.

162

16

The Divine and Demonic Natures

I N CHAPTER SIXTEEN THE LORD defines both the transcendental nature with its attendant qualities and the demonic nature with its accompanying qualities. He also explains the advantages of divine qualities and the disadvantages of demonic ones. He begins with the qualities that promote spiritual progress and liberation from the material world.

The Supreme Person
"Fearlessness, purification of one's existence, cultivation of spiritual knowledge, charity, self-control, performance of sacrifice, study of the *Vedas*, austerity, simplicity, nonviolence, truthfulness, freedom from anger, renunciation, tranquility, aversion to faultfinding, compassion for all, freedom from covetousness, gentleness, modesty, steady determination, vigor, forgiveness, fortitude, cleanliness, and freedom from envy and from the passion for honor—these transcendental qualities, O son of Pandu, belong to godly people endowed with divine nature."

Next, the Lord describes the royal road to hell: "Pride, arrogance, conceit, anger, harshness, and ignorance—these qualities belong to those of demonic nature, O Arjuna." Ungodly people desire worship and demand respect, although they do not command it. Over trifles they

As foam is created by the movements of a wave, atheists believe everything is created from the interaction of physical elements. In this chapter, Krishna describes the behavior of atheists who hold this view.

Right: A story has it that a frog, when informed of the vast ocean beyond his well, began to puff himself up to become as great as that ocean. With each puff he was told that the ocean was still greater than he, until at last, in his final effort, he burst. Similarly, atheists may deny and defy God, but in the end they encounter God as death and lose everything.

Below: Theists see that there is craftsmanship even in a leaf. Such intricacy, they know, has not happened by chance; a magnificent brain conceived its creation.

Left: Chemicals—like citric acid—are produced from life, not vice versa.

become angry and speak harshly. They don't know what should and what should not be done. They do everything whimsically, according to their own desires, and they do not recognize any authority.

"The transcendental qualities are conducive to liberation, whereas the demonic qualities make for bondage. Do not worry, O son of Pandu, for you are born with the divine qualities." Arjuna's involvement in the fight was not demonic because he was weighing the pros and cons— whether respectable persons should be killed or not—so he was acting above the influences of anger, false prestige, and malice.

"O Arjuna, in this world there are two kinds of created beings. One is called divine and the other demonic. I have already explained to you at length the divine qualities. Now hear from Me of the demonic.

"Those who are demonic do not know what is to be done and what is not to be done. Neither cleanliness nor proper behavior nor truth is found in them. They say that this world is unreal, with no foundation, no God in control. They say it is produced of sex desire and has no cause other than lust." For the demonic, matter combined with itself to produce living entities, and the soul does not exist. Material nature is the only cause of this manifestation. They have their own theories about the creation of the world.

"Following such conclusions, the demonic, who are lost to themselves and who have no intelligence, engage in unbeneficial, horrible works meant to destroy the world. Taking shelter of insatiable lust and absorbed in the conceit of pride and false prestige, the demonic, thus illusioned, are always sworn to unclean work, attracted by the impermanent."

The demonic try to enjoy this material world to the utmost limit and therefore always engage in inventing something for their sensory gratification. Such materialistic inventions are considered to reflect advancement of human civilization, but the true result is that people grow increasingly violent and cruel—cruel to animals as well as to other humans. They have no idea how to behave toward one another. Indirectly, Krishna's words anticipate the invention of nuclear weapons, created solely for mass destruction. Due to godlessness such weapons have been invented, as they are not meant for world peace or prosperity.

"The demonic believe that to gratify the senses is the prime necessity of human civilization. Thus until the end of life their anxiety is immeasurable. Bound by a network of hundreds of thousands of desires and absorbed in lust and anger, they secure money by illegal means for sense gratification." The demonic believe that the enjoyment of the senses is the ultimate goal of life, and they become more and more attracted to two things—sex enjoyment and accumulation of material wealth. And although they are gliding toward a hellish future, they consider themselves advanced. They do not believe in life after death, and they do not believe that one acquires different types of bodies according to one's karma, or activities in this world.

"The demonic person thinks: 'So much wealth do I have today, and I will gain more according to my schemes. So much is mine now, and it will increase in the future, more and more. He is my enemy, and I have killed him, and my other enemies will also be killed. I am the lord of everything. I am the enjoyer. I am perfect, powerful, and happy. I am the

Weapons of mass destruction are spawned from the demonic mentality.

Throughout the world, people with divine natures and those with demonic natures reside side by side. In this chapter Krishna distinguishes them by their qualities.

richest person, surrounded by aristocratic relatives. There is none so powerful and happy as I am. I shall perform sacrifices, give some charity, and thus rejoice.' " In this way such a person is deluded by ignorance.

"Thus perplexed by various anxieties and bound by a network of illusions, they become too strongly attached to sense enjoyment and fall down into hell."

Demonic people are enamored by the possessions they already have, such as land, family, house, and bank balance, and they are always planning to improve them. They believe in their own strength, and they do not know that their gains are due to their past good deeds. A competitor of such demonic persons is their enemy. There are many demonic people, and each is an enemy to the others. This enmity becomes deeper and deeper— between persons, then between families, then societies, and at last between nations. Therefore there is constant strife, war, and enmity throughout the world.

"Bewildered by false ego, strength, pride, lust, and anger, the demons become envious of the Supreme Person, who is in their own bodies and in the bodies of others, and blaspheme against the real religion."

Being envious of the scriptures and of the Supreme Lord, the demonic put forward false arguments against the existence of God and deny the scriptural authority.

"Those who are envious and mischievous, who are the lowest among people, I perpetually cast into the ocean of material existence, into various demonic species of life."

Demonic persons may not agree to accept the supremacy of the Lord, and they may act according to their own whims, but their next birth will depend upon the decision of the Supreme Lord rather than upon themselves. By the arrangement of the superior power, the demonic are perpetually put into the wombs of demons, and thus they continue to be envious, full of lust, always violent, hateful, and unclean.

"Attaining repeated birth amongst the species of demonic life, O Arjuna, such persons can never approach Me. Gradually they sink down to the most abominable type of existence.

"There are three gates leading to this hell—lust, anger, and greed. Every sane person should give these up, for they lead to the degradation of the soul. The person who has escaped these three gates of hell, O Arjuna, performs acts conducive to self-realization and thus gradually attains the supreme destination.

"Those who discard scriptural injunctions and act according to their own whims attain neither perfection, nor happiness, nor the supreme destination. One should therefore understand what is duty and what is not duty by the regulations of the scriptures. Knowing such rules and regulations, one should act to be gradually elevated." As stated in Chapter Fifteen, all the rules and regulations of the scriptures are intended for knowing Krishna. If we understand Krishna from the *Gita* and become situated in Krishna consciousness, engaging ourselves in devotional service, we have reached the perfection of knowledge.

Behind every arrangement—
large or small—is an arranger.

17

The Divisions of Faith

ARJUNA WONDERS ABOUT those who follow rules not mentioned in the scriptures and who have misguided faith in pseudo-gods and gurus.

Arjuna
"O Krishna, what is the situation of those who do not follow the principles of scripture but worship according to their own imaginations? Are they in goodness, in passion, or in ignorance?"

The Supreme Person
"According to the modes of nature acquired by the embodied soul, one's faith can be of three kinds—in goodness, in passion, or in ignorance. Now hear about this.

"O son of Pandu, according to one's existence under the various modes of nature, one evolves a particular kind of faith. The living being is said to be of a particular faith according to the modes it has acquired. People in the mode of goodness worship the demigods; those in the mode of passion worship the demons; and those in the mode of ignorance worship the ghosts and spirits." Every living being is a fragmental portion of the

The spirit soul is like a spark coming from a great fire. When the spark falls on dry grass, it easily ignites. Dry grass is likened to the mode of goodness, in which God consciousness readily awakens. When a spark falls on damp ground (which is likened to passion), it may or may not ignite. And if it falls on water (likened to ignorance), it surely will not ignite.

Supreme Lord. Therefore, originally we are transcendental to the modes of material nature. But when we forget our eternal relationship with the Supreme Lord, we become conditioned by goodness, passion, and ignorance, and we create our own situations due to our association with those different varieties of material nature. The resultant artificial faith is simply material.

"Even the food each person prefers is of three kinds, according to the three modes of material nature. The same is true of sacrifices, austerities, and charity. Now hear of the distinctions between them.

"Foods dear to those in the mode of goodness increase the duration of life, purify one's existence, and give strength, health, happiness, and satisfaction. Such foods are juicy, fatty, wholesome, and pleasing to the heart."

Foods that best promote health and increase life's duration, such as milk products, grains, fruits, and vegetables, are dear to those in the mode of goodness. Fatty foods have no connection with animal fat obtained by slaughter. Milk, butter, cheese, and the like give animal fat without the deaths of innocent creatures. Protein is amply available through legumes, whole wheat, other grains, and various food combinations.

"Foods that are too bitter, too sour, salty, hot, pungent, dry, and burning are dear to those in the mode of passion. Such foods cause distress, misery, and disease.

"Food prepared more than three hours before being eaten, food that is tasteless, decomposed and putrid, and food consisting of remnants and untouchable things is dear to those in the mode of darkness." Remnants of food may be eaten only when they are part of a meal that was first offered to the Supreme Lord or first eaten by a saintly person. Otherwise, the remnants of food are in the mode of darkness, and they increase disease.

"Of sacrifices, the sacrifice performed according to the directions of scripture, as a matter of duty, by those who desire no reward, is of the nature of goodness. But sacrifice performed for some material benefit, or for the sake of pride, O Arjuna, you should know to be in the mode of passion. Any sacrifice performed without regard for the directions of

By nature's arrangement, carnivorous animals have teeth suited for penetrating and tearing flesh. Human teeth are similar to those of plant-eaters— monkeys, elephants, and cows.

scripture, without distribution of spiritual food, without chanting of Vedic hymns and remunerations to the priests, and without faith is considered to be in the mode of ignorance."

The Supreme Lord then explains different kinds of austerity, penance, and charity. "Austerity of the body consists in worship of the Supreme Lord, the *brahmanas*, the spiritual master, and superiors like the father and mother, and in cleanliness, simplicity, celibacy, and nonviolence. Austerity of speech consists in speaking words that are truthful, pleasing, beneficial, and not agitating to others, and also in regularly reciting the Vedic literature. And satisfaction, simplicity, gravity, self-control, and purification of one's existence are the austerities of the mind." Austerity for the mind is detachment from sense gratification. When we free our minds from the pursuit of sense enjoyment, only then can we achieve true satisfaction. We should train our minds to think of the welfare of others.

"This threefold austerity, performed with transcendental faith by people not expecting material benefits but engaged only for the sake of the Supreme, is called austerity in goodness.

"Penance performed out of pride and for the sake of gaining respect, honor, and worship is said to be in the mode of passion. It is neither stable nor permanent.

"Penance performed out of foolishness, with self-torture or to destroy or injure others, is said to be in the mode of ignorance.

Penance performed through self-torture and without regard to scriptural guidelines is in the mode of ignorance.

179

"Charity given out of duty, without expectation of return, at the proper time and place, and to a worthy person is considered to be in the mode of goodness. But charity performed with the expectation of some return, or with a desire for fruitive results, or in a grudging mood, is said to be charity in the mode of passion. And charity performed at an impure place, at an improper time, to unworthy persons, or without proper attention and respect is said to be in the mode of ignorance."

Krishna has explained that penance, sacrifice, charity, and foods are divided into three categories: the modes of goodness, passion, and ignorance. But whether first class, second class, or third class, all these activities and substances are conditioned—contaminated by the material modes of nature.

"From the beginning of creation, the three words *om tat sat* were used to indicate the Supreme Absolute Truth. These three symbolic representations were used by *brahmanas* while chanting the hymns of the *Vedas* and during sacrifices for the satisfaction of the Supreme."

"Therefore, transcendentalists undertaking performances of sacrifice, charity, and penance according to scriptural regulations begin always with *om*, to attain the Supreme." When we direct penance, sacrifice, charity, and foods to the Supreme Lord they become means for spiritual elevation. We should perform all activities for the Supreme Lord, and thus become freed from the influence of material nature.

"Without desire for fruitive results, one should perform various kinds of sacrifice, penance, and charity with the word *tat*. The purpose of such transcendental activities is to get free from material entanglement.

"The Absolute Truth is the objective of devotional sacrifice, and it is indicated by the word *sat*. The performer of such sacrifice is also called *sat*, as are all works of sacrifice, penance, and charity which, true to the absolute nature, are performed to please the Supreme Person, O Arjuna.

Love of God is already dormant in everyone's heart and simply needs to be evoked. But we are always free to ignore this opportunity, as we are free to avoid the sunshine.

"Anything done as sacrifice, charity, or penance without faith in the Supreme, O Arjuna, is impermanent. It is called *asat* and is useless both in this life and the next." Krishna consciousness means acting solely for the pleasure of the Supreme. One who acts directly in Krishna consciousness transcends all three modes of material nature. To achieve this, we must first find the proper spiritual master and learn from that person. Then we can achieve faith in the Supreme. When that faith matures, in due course of time, it is called love of God. This love is the ultimate goal of all living entities.

18

Conclusion—The Perfection of Renunciation

As Chapter Two was a synopsis of the *Bhagavad-gita*, so Chapter Eighteen is a summary of all the topics discussed. In this chapter Lord Krishna reveals the purpose of life—to renounce material desires, to attain the transcendental position above the modes of material nature, and to engage in His devotional service.

Arjuna
"O mighty-armed one, I wish to understand the purpose of renunciation and of the renounced order of life."

The Supreme Lord
"The giving up of activities that are based on material desire is what great learned people call the renounced order of life. And giving up the results of all activities is what the wise call renunciation.

"Acts of sacrifice, charity and penance are not to be given up; they must be performed. Indeed, sacrifice, charity and penance purify even the great souls. All these activities should be performed without any

If a person uses a stick to strike a snake, that person is responsible for the act, not the stick itself. In the same way, when we fully dedicate ourselves to pleasing the Lord, we become His instruments. The Lord then takes charge in all our acts and frees us from all sins.

attachment or any expectation of result. They should be performed as a matter of duty, O son of Pandu. That is My final opinion."

We should relinquish sacrifices meant for material advancement, as their results are only temporary and further bind us to the illusory nature of material life. But sacrifices which purify our existence will elevate us to the spiritual plane. Devotees of the Lord accept any kind of work, sacrifice, or charity that will help them in the discharge of devotional service to the Lord and increase their Krishna consciousness.

"O best of the Pandavas, now hear My judgment about renunciation. The scriptures declare renunciation to be of three kinds. If one gives up one's prescribed duties because of illusion, such renunciation is said to be in the mode of ignorance. Prescribed duties should never be renounced." Work for material satisfaction will not advance us on the spiritual path. But activities such as cooking and offering the food to the Supreme Lord and then eating the remnants of such offerings, inspire us to more spiritual activity and should never be renounced.

"Those who give up prescribed duties as troublesome or out of fear of bodily discomfort have renounced in the mode of passion. Such action never leads to the elevation of renunciation." A Krishna conscious person does not renounce earning money from fear of performing fruitive

When friends and relatives gather at a crematorium, they often reflect, "One day our bodies will also be burnt to ashes. Why are we working so hard? What is the use of it all?" With these thoughts they become renounced, but influenced by material desires born of passion and ignorance, they quickly forget their renunciation.

activities. If by working we can engage our money in the service of God, or if by rising early in the morning we can advance our God consciousness, we must conquer over our mental resistance and feelings of inconvenience.

"O Arjuna, when people perform their prescribed duties only because they ought to be done, and renounce all material association and all attachment to the fruits, their renunciation is in the mode of goodness." The Lord's devotees act without attachment to the results of their activities. They dissociate from the material modes of work. Thus Krishna conscious office workers do not identify with the work of the office, nor with the workers in the office. They simply work for Krishna, and by giving the results of their work to Krishna, they are acting transcendentally.

"It is indeed impossible for an embodied being to give up all activities. But one who renounces the fruits of action is truly renounced. For one who is not renounced, the threefold fruits of action—desirable [heavenly], undesirable [hellish], and mixed—accrue after death. But those who are in the renounced order of life have no such results to suffer or enjoy.

"O mighty-armed Arjuna, according to the *Vedanta* there are five causes for the accomplishment of all action. Now learn of these from Me: the field of action [the body], the performer, the various senses, the many different kinds of endeavor, and ultimately the Supersoul—these are the five factors of action. Whatever right or wrong action a person performs by body, mind, or speech is caused by these five factors. Therefore one who thinks oneself the only doer, not considering the five factors, is certainly not very intelligent and cannot see things as they are.

"Those who are not motivated by false ego, whose intelligence is not entangled, though they kill people in this world, do not kill. Nor are such persons bound by their actions." Anyone who acts in Krishna consciousness under the direction of the Supersoul or the Supreme Person, even though killing, does not kill. Nor is such a person ever affected by the reaction of such killing. When a soldier kills under the command of a superior officer, he is not subject to being judged. But if a soldier kills on his own behalf, then he is accountable and will be judged in a court of law.

"According to the three different modes of material nature, there are three kinds of knowledge, work, and workers. Now hear of them from Me.

"That knowledge by which one undivided spiritual nature is seen in all living entities, though they are divided into innumerable forms, you should understand to be in the mode of goodness." A person who sees one spirit soul in every living being, whether a human, animal, bird, beast, aquatic, or plant, possesses knowledge in the mode of goodness. One spirit soul is in each living being, although each has a different body determined by its previous work. As described in Chapter Seven, the manifestation of the living force in every body is due to the superior nature of the Supreme Lord. That living force is imperishable, although the body is perishable. Because many types of material bodies exist in conditioned life, the living force may appear to be divided, but to be able to perceive that living force as one superior nature in every body is to see in the mode of goodness. Such impersonal knowledge is one aspect of self-realization.

"That knowledge by which one sees that in every different body there is a different type of living entity you should understand to be in the mode of passion."

The idea that the material body is the living entity and that with the destruction of the body also comes the annihilation of consciousness is called knowledge in the mode of passion.

A God conscious person sees the hand of the Lord behind everything. Not a blade of grass moves without His will.

In the mode of goodness one may think that at liberation the soul merges into an all-pervasive eternal light. Yet Krishna declares that the soul never loses its individuality. A bird may seem to merge into a tree, but in fact the bird still exists. (Follow the pointer up.)

"And that knowledge by which one is attached to one kind of work as the all in all, without knowledge of the truth, and which is very meager, is said to be in the mode of darkness." For a person in the mode of ignorance, God is money, and knowledge means the satisfaction of bodily demands.

To summarize, knowledge concerning the spirit soul which is transcendent to this mortal body is called knowledge in the mode of goodness; knowledge producing many theories and doctrines by dint of mundane logic and mental speculation is the product of the mode of passion; and knowledge concerned only with keeping the body comfortable is said to be in the mode of ignorance.

"That action which is regulated and which is performed without attachment, without love or hatred, and without desire for fruitive results is said to be in the mode of goodness.

"But action performed with great effort by one seeking to gratify one's desires, and enacted from a sense of false ego, is called action in the mode of passion. That action performed in illusion, in disregard of scriptural injunctions, and without concern for future bondage or for violence or distress caused to others is in the mode of ignorance.

"One who performs one's duty without association with the modes of material nature, without false ego, with great determination and enthusiasm, and without wavering in success or failure is a worker in the mode of goodness.

"The worker who is attached to work and the fruits of work, desiring to enjoy those fruits, and who is greedy, always envious, impure, and moved by joy and sorrow is in the mode of passion.

"The worker who is always engaged in work against the injunctions of the scripture, who is materialistic, obstinate, cheating, and expert in insulting others, and who is lazy, always morose, and procrastinating is a worker in the mode of ignorance.

"O Arjuna, now please listen as I tell you in detail of the different kinds of understanding and determination, according to the three modes of material nature.

"That understanding by which one knows what ought to be done and what ought not to be done, what is to be feared and what is not to be feared, what is binding and what is liberating is in the mode of goodness.

"That understanding which cannot distinguish between religion

A worker in the mode of passion is absorbed in self-created burdens, but at last death ends all his efforts, just as the tide washes away even an elaborate sandcastle.

and irreligion, between action that should be done and action that should not be done, is in the mode of passion. That understanding which considers irreligion to be religion and religion to be irreligion, under the spell of illusion and darkness, and strives always in the wrong direction is in the mode of ignorance.

"That determination which is unbreakable, which is sustained with steadfastness by yoga practice, and which thus controls the activities of the mind, life, and senses is determination in the mode of goodness. But that determination by which one holds fast to fruitive results in religion, economic development, and sense gratification is of the nature of passion, O Arjuna. And that determination which cannot go beyond dreaming, fearfulness, lamentation, moroseness, and illusion—such unintelligent determination is in the mode of darkness.

"O best of the Pandavas, now please hear from Me about the three kinds of happiness by which the conditioned souls enjoy, and by which they sometimes come to the end of all distress.

"That which in the beginning may be just like poison but at the end is just like nectar and which awakens one to self-realization is said to be happiness in the mode of goodness." In the pursuit of self-realization, we need to follow many rules and regulations to control the mind and senses and to concentrate the mind on the self. All these procedures are difficult, often even bitter like poison, but if we succeed in following the regulations and attain the transcendental position, we begin to drink real nectar and enjoy life.

"That happiness which is derived from contact of the senses with their objects and which appears like nectar at first but poison at the end is of the nature of passion. And that happiness which is blind to self-realization, which is delusion from beginning to end and which arises from sleep, laziness, and illusion is of the nature of ignorance.

The happiness one gets from society, friendship, and love is like a drop of water in the desert. In the vast desert, one drop of water is insignificant. Similarly, material happiness is insignificant. It cannot satisfy one's innermost desire for spiritual pleasure.

"There is no being existing, either here or among the demigods in the higher planetary systems, who is free from these three modes of material nature.

"*Brahmanas* [learned and pious teachers], *kshatriyas* [military fighters and governmental administrators], *vaisyas* [farmers and merchants], and *sudras* [laborers] are distinguished by the qualities born of their own natures in accordance with the material modes, O chastiser of the enemy.

"Peacefulness, self-control, austerity, purity, tolerance, honesty, knowledge, wisdom, and religiousness—these are the natural qualities by which the *brahmanas* work.

"Heroism, power, determination, resourcefulness, courage in battle, generosity, and leadership are the natural qualities of work for the *kshatriyas*.

"Farming, cow protection, and business are the natural work for the *vaisyas*, and for the *sudras* there is labor as well as service to others.

"By working according to one's nature, everyone can become perfect. Now please hear from Me how this can be done.

"By worship of the Lord, who is the source of all beings and who is all-pervading, people can attain perfection through performing their own work." We should think that we are engaged occupationally by the Supreme Lord, the master of the senses. And with the results of the work in which we are engaged, we should worship the Supreme Lord. In this way the Supreme Lord Himself will take charge of delivering us, and by His mercy we will achieve the highest perfection.

"It is better to engage in one's own occupation, even though one may perform it imperfectly, than to accept another's occupation and perform it perfectly. Duties prescribed according to one's nature are never affected by sinful reactions." We should not imitate another's duty. A person who is by nature attracted to the kind of work done by *sudras* should not artificially claim to be a *brahmana*, although that person may have been born into a *brahmana* family. In this way, one should work according to one's own nature; no work is abominable, if performed in the service of the Supreme Lord. Whether one is a *brahmana*, a *kshatriya*, a *vaisya*, or a *sudra* doesn't matter if one serves the Supreme Lord by one's work. But anything done for personal sense gratification is a cause of bondage. The

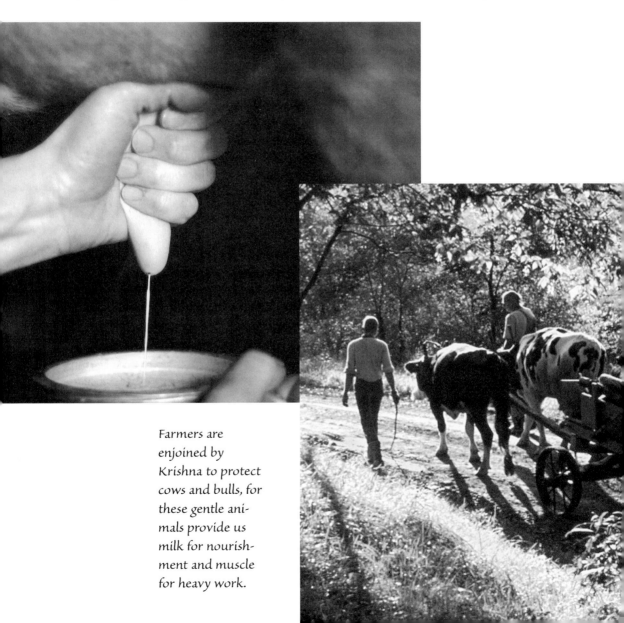

Farmers are enjoined by Krishna to protect cows and bulls, for these gentle animals provide us milk for nourishment and muscle for heavy work.

conclusion is that we all should work according to the particular modes of nature we have acquired and should decide to work only to serve the supreme cause of the Supreme Lord.

"Every endeavor is covered by some fault, just as fire is covered by smoke. Therefore you should not give up the work born of your nature, even if such work is full of fault." We must not give up our natural occupations due to disturbing elements, but rather continue in our work, fixed in our determination to serve the Supreme Lord.

"Those who are self-controlled and unattached and who disregard all material enjoyments can obtain, by practice of renunciation, the perfect stage of freedom from reaction."

Renunciation means that we are always thinking of ourselves as parts and parcels of the Supreme Lord, and are therefore aware that the results of our work belong only to Him. This is God consciousness. With this mentality, we are satisfied because we are acting for the Supreme. Thus we become attached to the spiritual; we become accustomed to taking pleasure in the transcendental happiness derived from the service of the Lord.

"O son of Pandu, learn from Me how one who has achieved this perfection can attain the supreme perfectional stage [Brahman], the stage of highest knowledge, by acting in the way I shall now summarize."

The Lord describes for Arjuna how he can achieve the perfectional stage simply by being engaged in his occupational duty and by performing that duty for the Supreme Lord. "Being purified by one's intelligence and controlling the mind with determination, giving up the objects of sense gratification, being freed from attachment and hatred, one who lives in a secluded place, who eats little, who controls the body, mind, and power of speech, who is always in trance, and who is detached, free from false ego, false strength, false pride, lust, anger, and acceptance of material things, free from false proprietorship, and peaceful—such a person is certainly elevated to the position of self-realization.

Although full of smoke, fire still does its work of burning. In the same way, though our efforts may be flawed, we can still serve the Supreme Lord by our work.

"One who is thus transcendentally situated at once realizes the Supreme Absolute Truth and becomes fully joyful. Such a person never laments or desires to have anything and is equally disposed toward every living entity. In that state one attains pure devotional service unto Me."

The devotee in God consciousness laments for nothing nor desires for anything. Since God is full, the living entities who are engaged in His service also become full in themselves. Because pure devotees see everything in relation to God, they are naturally always joyful. They do not see persons in the material world as higher or lower than one another; higher and lower positions are ephemeral, and devotees disregard ephemeral appearances and disappearances.

"One can understand Me as I am, as the Supreme Person, only by devotional service. And when one is in full consciousness of Me by such devotion, one can enter into the kingdom of God." If we want to understand the Supreme Lord, we have to undertake pure devotional service under the guidance of a pure devotee. Otherwise, the truth of the Supreme Lord will always be hidden. No one can understand God simply by erudite scholarship or mental speculation. Only one who is actually engaged in Krishna consciousness and devotional service can understand who and what Krishna is. And one who is fully conversant with the science of Krishna becomes eligible to enter into the spiritual kingdom, the eternal, transcendental abode of Krishna.

"Though engaged in all kinds of activities, My pure devotee, under My protection, reaches the eternal and imperishable abode by My grace. In all activities just depend upon Me and work always under My protection. In such devotional service, be fully conscious of Me."

We may argue that Arjuna was acting under the personal instruction of Krishna, but when Krishna does not appear to be present (to those of us who cannot perceive Him at all times), then how should we act? If we act according to the direction of Krishna in the *Bhagavad-gita*, as well as under the guidance of Krishna's bona fide representatives, then the results will be the same. We should have no goal in life except acting in Krishna consciousness just to satisfy Krishna. And while acting in this way, we should think of Krishna only, in the knowledge that we have

As the fingers naturally serve the body and
become vitalized, the soul wants to serve
the Supreme Soul and become fulfilled.

been appointed by Krishna to discharge these particular duties. While acting in such a way, we naturally have to think of Krishna. This is perfect Krishna consciousness. We cannot, however, act whimsically and then offer the results to the Supreme Lord. That sort of duty is not devotional service to the Lord.

"If you become conscious of Me, you will pass over all the obstacles of conditioned life by My grace. If, however, you do not work in such consciousness but act through false ego, not hearing Me, you will be lost. If you do not act according to My direction and do not fight, then you will be falsely directed. By your nature you will have to be engaged in warfare. Under illusion you are now declining to act according to My direction. But, compelled by the work born of your own nature, you will act all the same, O Arjuna." If we refuse to act under the Supreme Lord's direction, then the modes in which we are situated compel us to act. Everyone is under the spell of changeable combinations of the modes of nature, and is acting accordingly. But those who voluntarily engage themselves under the direction of the Supreme Lord become glorious.

"The Supreme Lord is situated in everyone's heart, O Arjuna, and is directing the wanderings of all living entities, who are seated as on a machine, made of the material energy. Surrender unto Him utterly. By His grace you will attain transcendental peace and the supreme and eternal abode." The Supreme Lord, as the localized Supersoul, sits in the heart, directing the living being. Upon changing bodies, the living entity

When Krishna spoke the *Bhagavad-gita* thousands of years ago, He described the body as a machine made of material energy. Today this is confirmed, as bodily organs and limbs—the heart, lungs, legs, and so on—are sometimes replaced by other machines. The machine of the human body is designed by the Lord to enable the living entity to function in this world and, at the same time, become spiritually elevated.

forgets its past deeds, but the Supersoul, as the knower of the past, present, and future, remains the witness of all the soul's activities. Therefore, all the activities of a living entity are directed by the Supersoul. The living entity gets what it deserves—the results of its actions—and is carried by the material body, which is created from the material energy under the direction of the Supersoul. As soon as a living entity is placed in a particular type of body, it must work under the spell of that bodily situation. One must, therefore, surrender unto the Supreme Person; that will relieve one from all kinds of miseries of this material existence and, at the end, will enable one to reach the Supreme Lord.

"Thus I have explained to you knowledge still more confidential. Deliberate on this fully, and then do what you wish to do." God does not interfere with the little independence of the living entity. Surrender to the Supreme Lord is in the best interest of the living entities. It is not for the interest of the Supreme. Before surrendering, we are free to deliberate on this subject as far as our intelligence takes us; that is the best way to come to accept the instruction of the Supreme Lord. Such instruction comes through the spiritual master, the bona fide representative of Krishna.

"Because you are My very dear friend, I am speaking to you My supreme instruction, the most confidential knowledge of all. Hear this from Me, for it is for your benefit. Always think of Me, become My devotee, worship Me, and offer your homage unto Me. Thus you will come to Me without fail. I promise you this because you are My very dear friend."

This is the essence of the teachings of the *Bhagavad-gita*; it cannot be understood by a common person, but only by one who is very dear to Krishna—His pure devotee. In the human form of life we have the opportunity and the free will to mold our lives so that we can simply think of Krishna. This is the most important instruction in all Vedic literature, the most essential part of knowledge—meant not only for Arjuna, but for all living entities. Whoever follows the path of Arjuna can become a dear friend to Krishna and obtain the same perfection as Arjuna.

"Abandon all varieties of religion and just surrender unto Me. I shall deliver you from all sinful reactions. Do not fear."

In summarizing the *Bhagavad-gita*, the Lord requests Arjuna to give up all the processes of knowledge and religion that have been explained to him and choose simply to surrender to Krishna. That surrender will save him from all kinds of sinful reactions, for the Lord personally promises to protect him. We may think that, unless we are free from all sinful reactions, we cannot surrender to God. Addressing such doubts Krishna states that, even if we are not free from all sinful reactions, simply by surrendering to Him, we are freed automatically. Even through the most herculean efforts, we cannot rid ourselves of our sinful reactions and our entanglement in the cycle of birth and death. We simply must unhesitatingly accept Krishna as the supreme savior of all living entities. With faith and love we should surrender unto Him.

We may perform any particular occupational duty according to our situation in the modes of material nature, but if by executing this duty we do not come to the point of God consciousness, all our activities are in vain. Anything not leading to the perfectional stage of God consciousness is a waste of the valuable time we have in the human form of life.

There are different kinds of transcendentalists—some are attached to the impersonal Brahman vision, some are attracted by the Supersoul feature, and so forth. But those who are attracted to the personal Supreme Lord, Krishna Himself, are the most perfect transcendentalists. In other

Just as actors appear to have enemies or to suffer, but actually don't, so spiritually advanced persons realize that they actually have no enemies or miseries.

words, devotional service to Krishna, in full Krishna consciousness, is the most confidential and intimate part of knowledge, and this is the essence of the whole *Bhagavad-gita.* We may be perplexed as to how we can give up all forms of religion and simply surrender to Krishna, but such worry is useless.

"This confidential knowledge may never be explained to those who are not austere, or devoted, or engaged in devotional service, nor to one who is envious of Me." Many persons envy Krishna because He has explained in the *Bhagavad-gita* that He is the Supreme and that nothing is above Him or equal to Him. Such persons should not hear the *Bhagavad-gita* for they cannot understand it and Krishna.

"For those who explain this supreme secret [knowledge of Krishna] to the devotees, pure devotional service is guaranteed, and at the end they will come back to Me. There are no servants in this world more dear to Me than they, nor will there ever be ones more dear. And I declare that those who study this sacred conversation of ours worship Me by their intelligence. And those who listen with faith and without envy become free from sinful reactions and attain to the auspicious planets where the pious dwell.

"O Arjuna, have you heard this with an attentive mind? And are your ignorance and illusions now dispelled?"

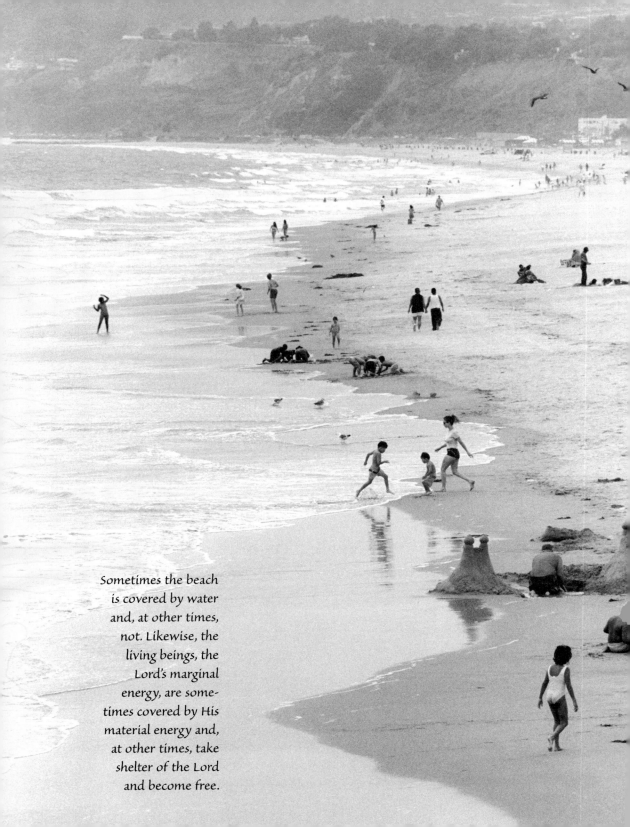

Sometimes the beach is covered by water and, at other times, not. Likewise, the living beings, the Lord's marginal energy, are sometimes covered by His material energy and, at other times, take shelter of the Lord and become free.

Arjuna

"My dear Krishna, O infallible one, my illusion is now gone. I have regained my memory by Your mercy. I am now firm and free from doubt and am prepared to act according to Your instructions."

Sanjaya

"Thus I have heard the conversation of two great souls, Krishna and Arjuna. And so wonderful is that message that my hair is standing on end.

"By the mercy of my spiritual master, Vyasa, I have heard these most confidential talks directly from the master of all mysticism, Krishna, who was speaking personally to Arjuna. O Dhritarastra, as I repeatedly recall this wondrous and holy dialogue between Krishna and Arjuna, I take pleasure, being thrilled at every moment. As I remember the wonderful universal form of Lord Krishna, I am struck with wonder more and more, and I rejoice again and again.

"Wherever there is Krishna, the master of all mystics, and wherever there is Arjuna, the supreme archer, there will also certainly be opulence, victory, extraordinary power, and morality. That is my opinion."

The *Bhagavad-gita* began with Dhritarastra's inquiry. He was hopeful of victory for his sons, assisted by great warriors. However, after describing the scene on the battlefield, Sanjaya told Dhritarastra, "You are thinking of victory, but my opinion is that where Krishna and Arjuna are present, there will be all good fortune." Dhritarastra could not expect victory for his side.

Bhagavad-gita is the supreme instruction in religion and morality: become a devotee of Krishna and surrender unto Him. As minute parts and parcels of Krishna, the living entities have a tendency to be in contact with either the material energy or the spiritual energy. In other words, the living entities are situated between the two energies of the Lord, and because they belong to the superior energy of the Lord, they have a particle of independence. By proper use of that independence, they receive the supreme directive of Krishna. Thus they realize their natural and original state of immortality, knowledge, and transcendental happiness.